LIFE IN CHRIST

BY THE SAME AUTHOR

THE ELEMENTS OF THE SPIRITUAL LIFE

A Study in Ascetical Theology

WITH AN INTRODUCTION BY

THE RIGHT REV.

MARK CARPENTER-GARNIER, D.D.
Bishop of Colombo

Fourth Impression

10s. 6d.

SOCIETY FOR PROMOTING CHRISTIAN
KNOWLEDGE

LIFE IN CHRIST

BY

F. P. HARTON, B.D.

Fellow of King's College, London
Vicar of Baulking

A. R. MOWBRAY & Co. LIMITED
LONDON AND OXFORD
MOREHOUSE PUBLISHING CO.
NEW YORK AND MILWAUKEE

[1937]

First published in 1937

Printed in Great Britain

PREFACE

THAT the Christian is essentially a new creature whose life is not only for but in Christ is the teaching of the New Testament and the Fathers and spiritual teachers of the Church; nevertheless it has been and still is much obscured, so that, in some cases, Catholics tend to regard Christian living as little more than the exterior observance of the Church's precepts and Protestants to think of it as a human imitation of the perfect example of Christ. But if Christianity is to fulfil God's purpose for it in our distracted generation it seems to me that it is urgently necessary that Christians should realize the implications of their spiritual relationship to Christ in the Church, and it is these implications that I have attempted to elucidate in the following pages.

This book has been evolved out of two courses of sermons and no doubt it still bears some marks of its origin; nevertheless its purpose is neither homiletic nor hortatory, still less controversial; it is an attempt to explain to the ordinary Christian something of the fundamentals of his life and being, and as such I offer it to all who care for the things of God.

F. P. HARTON

Baulking
September, 1937

CONTENTS

LIFE IN CHRIST

CHAPTER I

SONS OF GOD

'Beloved, now are we the sons of God.'—1 S. JOHN iii. 2.

IF we are truly to understand what sort of life it is
that, as Christians, we should lead, we must first
of all inquire what it is that, as Christians, we are.
Christian spirituality rests upon the fact that when
God makes human beings members of His Church
in Holy Baptism He not only admits them into a
society of men, but also makes a radical change in
their very selves, so that it may truly be said that
'if any man is in Christ, he is a new creature,'[1] or,
as the Revised Version margin reads even more
cogently, 'there is a new creation.' Holy Baptism
is not only the doing away of sin so that the baptized
may be able to make a fresh start, though it is that,
it is a renewal of so radical a kind that it can be
described as a new creation, a making again.
S. Paul emphasizes this newness in many places, and
it is characteristic of the religion of the New Testament, but it is singularly little realized to-day : hence
much of the weakness of contemporary Christianity.

[1] 2 Cor. v. 17.

9

In Christianity we find more than a new revelation
of God, a new forgiveness, a new ethic, a new
Example; in the Church more than an aggregation
of believers. In the symbolism of Holy Baptism
S. Paul[1] sees not only 'a death unto sin,' but still
more 'newness of life,' comparable to and consequent
upon the risen life of our Lord; a new life of a new
being.

What are we then, we new creatures in Christ
Jesus? S. John gives us the answer in a sentence.
'Beloved,' he says, 'now are we the sons of God.'
That and nothing less than that.

He places first the little word 'now.' This implies
that we are something now, as Christians, which
we were not before. There is a sense in which it is
true to say that all men are the children of God and
not Christians only; He created all, He loves all.
He created all for Himself and desires that all should
enter into the fullness of sonship; nevertheless, all
men are not sons in the full sense of the word, and
they can only become so through union with the
eternal Son. The Christian is a son of God in the
fullest sense of the term, and he is so by virtue of the
gift of God in Baptism.

Further, S. John's 'now' implies that we all, even
the newly-baptized infant, really are sons of God.
The Apostle refuses to speculate about our future
state, 'it is not yet made manifest what we shall be.'
One thing he knows, that we are now sons of God.
We are not given merely the possibility of sonship
in heaven, we do not have sonship set before us as
the goal which we seek to attain on earth (our goal

[1] Rom. vi. 3 ff.; Col. iii. 1-3.

is something different from that), but we are sons
here and now, and all our life is changed by that
fact.

It was to make us sons of God that our Lord Jesus
Christ was born of Blessed Mary in Bethlehem. That
was the end and purpose of the Incarnation.
S. Athanasius puts the matter crisply when he says,
'The Son of God became son of man that the sons
of man, that is to say of Adam, might become sons
of God.'[1] That is not merely an epigram, it is the
enunciation of a fundamental truth. Our Lord did
not come into this world in order to help us, He
came to make us sons of God; that alone was the
full purpose of His coming, as S. John says in the
Prologue to his Gospel, 'As many as received Him,
to them gave He power to become the sons of God,
even to them that believe on His Name: which were
born, not of blood, nor of the will of the flesh, nor
of the will of man, but of God.'[2]

If, then, we are sons of God through Christ we
must try and understand what our sonship means,
for we do not necessarily understand an idea when
we perceive that it is true. For the beginnings of
this understanding we must go to S. Paul. 'When
the fullness of the time was come,' he says, 'God sent
forth His Son, made of a woman, made under the
law, to redeem them that were under the law, that
we might receive the adoption of sons.'[3] Several
important truths are contained in that short sentence,
but we are now concerned with only one of them,
indeed with one word, 'adoption.' Our Lord Jesus

[1] *de Incarnatione Dei Verbi* 8.   [2] S. John i. 12-13.
[3] Gal. iv. 4-5.

Christ is the eternal Son of God because He is of the
same nature as the Father, Very God of Very God, but
we are not like that; we are not God, and never can
be (to believe otherwise is to fall into the heresy of
Pantheism); we are creatures of God, wonderful
indeed, but finite and quite other than divine,
dependent for our being and our life upon the will
of Him Who made us.   Moreover, we are not only
creatures but fallen creatures, and our original likeness to our Creator is grievously smirched with sin.
How can such beings be, in any true sense, the sons
of God?   Obviously our sonship must be the result
of divine intervention, and that of a very special
kind; it is this intervention which S. Paul explains
by the term 'adoption.'

Now adoption, as we all know, is a legal process
whereby a man takes a child which is not his own
by birth and makes him his own, if we may so put
it, by grace.[1]   The child so adopted is not his own,
in the sense that his natural child is, and never will
be, but he is his child henceforward; his adoption
has given him a totally new status and made him
the son in all but birth of one who was not his father
until that new status was given.   If a king were to
adopt the son of a peasant that child would no
longer be a peasant but a prince, and a real prince;
just so, when God adopts us in Holy Baptism He
takes a son of man, who in comparison with the
divine majesty is infinitely lower than the humblest
peasant, and makes him His own son.

[1] If we take the word 'grace' in its simplest sense of
'favour' this statement is literally true, but we must not,
of course, confuse such 'grace' with the grace of God.

This means, in the first place, a new relationship
to God Himself; He is henceforward not only Deity
but Father, not only God but *my* God, a God known
not only by revelation but also by spiritual relationship, a God Who loves and wills to be loved in
return. It is a tremendous thing that God, taking
pity on human blindness, should reveal Himself to
men, and we can never be thankful enough for the
Christian revelation, for the coming of the true Light
into this dark world; but it is a vastly greater thing
that, in the Eternal Word, men should themselves
be united with God and enter into the knowledge of
His Fatherhood. A man may be a theist and yet
worship a very distant, cold, and impersonal Deity;
the Christian knows that God is, that He is Love,
that He is Father, because he himself is God's son,
and that makes the whole difference to life.

Then adoption is admittance into a new family.
There are families and families, into some we would
gladly enter and from others we would fain escape;
but no family is so glorious as the family of God,
that family which, however externally severed, is
one throughout the whole world, one with the souls
in purgatory and with the saints in heaven, essentially one now, to be actually one hereafter. To be
at home in that family is the gladdest birth-right
which can be inherited by man, and God has given
it to us. We, who are sinners, can be at home with
the saints, because we are all the children of
God.

More than this, God has, in adoption, restored to
us our lost inheritance. Man was created to know,
love, and serve God in this world and to be happy

with Him for ever in the next, but, like Esau, he
sold his birthright, not for a mess of pottage but for
something much less sustaining; by his own sin he
made himself incapable of fulfilling the end for which
God had created him, and wasted his substance, the
inheritance which God had prepared for him.   But
it is impossible for the will of God to remain per-
manently unfulfilled; the divine wisdom can repair
even the evil of sin, and in making men His sons
God does repair it, cleansing the soul from its guilt,
straightening the twists of original sin, making us
once more capable of attaining our end.

Grace is often spoken of as though it contradicted
nature; but it does not contradict nature, it completes it.   What it does contradict is sin.   By sin
the natural man has been deformed, but by grace
God once more makes him straight and capable of
perfection, a new man.   How wonderful is the divine
newness!

By adoption, then, God gives us a new status, a
new relationship to Himself, but the mystery of our
sonship does not end there.   S. Paul speaks in terms
of a legal process, something which is primarily a
matter of status and not of being; S. John takes us
further into the heart of the matter.

When Nicodemus came to visit Him, our Lord
met him with a categorical assertion which caused
him no little astonishment, for the Evangelist tells us
that 'Jesus answered and said unto him, Verily,
verily, I say unto thee, Except a man be born again,
he cannot see the kingdom of God,' and when His
interlocutor expressed his surprise at so remarkable
a statement He merely repeated it a little more

definitely, 'Except a man be born of water and of
the Spirit, he cannot enter into the kingdom of
God.'[1] This brings us face to face with the fact
that Baptism is something more than adoption into
the family of God; it is a veritable new birth from
above in which God through the agency of the Holy
Spirit becomes the Father of the baptized in a deeper
sense than that which we have just considered.
Adoption, as we have seen, alters the status of the
adopted, but a new birth signifies a change in his
very being, truly making him a 'new creature.' In
Baptism God infuses a new and supernatural element
into the soul's being, making it something that it was
not before; the reborn soul is therefore something
essentially greater than the adopted soul. This
being so, why should we not abandon the term
'adoption' in favour of the more comprehensive term
'new birth'?

This question raises an important consideration.
The supernatural infusion of which we are thinking
raises the soul above its natural self, making it poten-
tially a 'new man,' yet that supernatural elevation
does not destroy the 'old man,' as we know to our
cost in daily experience, but completes and reorientates it, and the conception of 'adoption' keeps this
fact before our minds. In spite of our new birth,
we are still creatures—and fallen creatures— adopted
into the family of God, and we need to keep this
fundamental humility if our 'old man' is to be
restored and perfected; but we are at the same time
children of God by a new birth, and a balanced

[1] S. John iii. 3, 5.

understanding of our condition must take account
of both factors, adoption and birth.

A true appreciation of the work of grace will never
allow us to depreciate nature. God has created us
all in His own image, capable of knowing and loving
Him (otherwise there could be no point of contact
between the creature and the Creator for Whom he
was made), and that likeness to, that capability for
God is inherent in us, though overlaid by sin, grace
or no grace. What God does in Baptism is to
restore and perfect that likeness by raising it to a
more radical resemblance. It is one thing to be
created in the image of God, it is another to be born
of Him. In the one case you have a likeness of
two dissimilar beings, the one infinitely inferior to
the other; in the second case you have the resemblance of a son to his father which comes from
community of nature, the one resembling the other
because he is his father's son. We are both creatures
and sons.

We have used the phrase 'community of nature,'
and this leads us into the heart of the mystery of
sonship. When a man begets a child he gives it not
only life but a certain participation in his own being;
it is not any sort of living thing which is born but
a man, not any sort of man but this man's son; just
so when we are born again of God we become God's
sons in the fullest possible sense, 'partakers of the
divine nature.'[1]

This fact comes to us to-day with a sense of shock;
we have grown so accustomed to an imperfect
realization of our condition as Christians that we find

[1] 2 S. Pet. i. 4.

it hard to believe in the fullness of our salvation, 'birth' means for us something much less than birth, and 'sonship' becomes merely equivalent to creature-liness. But with the Fathers it was not so, they realized these things for what they truly are. We looked above at the statement of S. Athanasius that 'the Son of God became son of man that the sons of men might become sons of God,' a statement that is echoed in the West by S. Leo[1] in almost identical terms; now we find S. Athanasius going much further in the words, 'He became man that we might be made God,'[2] and this again is echoed by S. Augustine.[3] The truth of our deification is part of the common teaching of the Church.

If this is so it is important that we should try and get as clear an idea as possible of what this deification means. It is clear that it does not mean that we are made gods in any absolute sense, such an idea is contradicted by experience and common sense. Certainly rather extravagant language has sometimes been used in this connection, particularly in commenting on such passages of Scripture as 'I have said, Ye are gods,' but the essential truth is clear enough. God gives us participation in His nature, not in His being. A child is the son of his father, but he is not his father; equally we are the sons of God, but we are not God. He is the eternal, infinite God; we are temporal, finite creatures and ever remain so, and it is this truth which the conception of adoption guards. But God deifies us by communicating His nature to us in such a way as it can

[1] *Serm. in Nat. Dom.* vi.   [2] *Oratio de Incarn. Verbi* 54.
[3] *Serm.* clxvi.

B

be assimilated by our humanity; the human element is always there but it is perfected and raised above itself by the divine.

In the Garden of Eden man sinned by desiring to become as God in his own right, so that he should leave behind the limitations of his humanity; he is saved by being made as God, not in his own right at all, not renouncing his creatureliness, but by living as a son of God and participating in that nature which is, and always must be, God's and not man's. This participation is a gift of divine grace and not our own, a gift which may be, and, alas, often is, neglected or misused. We have this treasure in earthen vessels, and a man who deliberately lives on the natural or animal level may lose all sense of God and descend to the lowest depths of evil, in spite of his participation of the divine nature, for God in His humility submits the operations of His grace to the hegemony of the human will. Nevertheless, the gift is there, and we shall have to answer for its use at the last day.

This deification consists primarily in the uniting of two beings who are and ever remain distinct, God and the human soul. The unity between father and son is a fundamental reality; the son may have many points of dissimilarity from his father, but he also has an essential likeness which is the fruit of his sonship, an essential oneness of nature. So it is with us, and all the manifold operations of divine grace and all the practice of Christian spirituality are directed towards the deepening of that unity. Grace is not a divine aid to the production of human virtues, it is the power of Christ which brings forth His

virtues in us, because by it we are already sharers
in the divine nature. In making us His sons God
unites Himself to our very being and disposes us not
merely to human but to divine operations.

In giving us this essential unity with His nature God
also gives us a new likeness to Himself. S. Thomas
Aquinas speaks of our condition as being 'nothing else
than a certain participated likeness to the divine
nature.'[1] Those words are very carefully chosen,
not in any way to minimize our deification, but to
guard our essential creatureliness and keep us
humble; 'a certain participated likeness' truly, but
a likeness notwithstanding and a very wonderful
one.

It is true in a sense to say that there is a certain
likeness to God in all creation, since all creation is
the fruit of His thought and creative will, and that
likeness becomes actual in those beings which are
likest Him in having a spiritual nature, in the angels
who are pure spirits and in man who is spirit and
flesh. So the statement in Genesis that man was
made in the image of God is quite true, but that
likeness is that of the thing made to Him Who made
it, the creature to the Creator Whose being is utterly
different to, and separate from, his own; we may
define it as a potential capacity for God, a capacity
upon which the Holy Spirit can work. There must
be such a likeness that there may be any sort of
contact between man and God; if man's spirit were
totally different from God his soul would be a closed
world, he could never reach out beyond his little
human circle; but because God has made him in

[1] *Summa Theologica* III, Q. lxii, art. 1.

His own image man, in virtue of his humanity, can seek after God and find Him, he has the capacity for knowing and loving, not only creation, but God. As S. Augustine says, 'Thou, O God, hast made [not only redeemed] us for Thyself.'[1]

But the likeness of the Christian to God is vastly greater than this, not the likeness of the creature to the Creator but the likeness of the son to the Father, a likeness springing from community of nature.

In giving us this God not only lifts us into the supernatural sphere, He supernaturalizes us, giving us not only a capacity for Himself but a fruition of that capacity the possibilities of which we can hardly guess at in this life; yet it is a possession in this life in the power of which we live here and now.

'Beloved, now are we the sons of God.' Let us then dare to live as His sons and realize something at least of the wonder and greatness of that redeemed being which, in His great love, He has given to us. We shall find much in us to contradict it, many ill-regulated desires, some positive evil, for if our best self is like God our worst self is still far from that likeness. But if we are truly sons we shall set ourselves with new vigour and a sure and certain hope to eradicate all that is unworthy of our sonship. We shall seek to love God not only because He is God, but because He is our Father, and loving Him we shall be His sons indeed.

[1] *Conf.* I, i.

CHAPTER II

MEMBERS OF CHRIST

'*I am the vine, ye are the branches: He that abideth in Me, and I in him, the same bringeth forth much fruit : for without Me ye can do nothing.*'—S. JOHN xv. 5.

IN the last chapter we considered what S. John—and, incidentally, the Church Catechism—tells us that we are as Christians. We were dealing with our being and its relation to the being of God—a somewhat metaphysical subject—and, since metaphysics is not a popular branch of knowledge, it is possible that some may find such considerations rather difficult. In this chapter we pass on to another truth of the Catechism which should be easier of comprehension.

The Catechism says that we are not only children of God but also members of Christ, a statement whose full value we seldom completely appreciate. It will be well, then, to think about this, for the two facts are closely interrelated. We are sons of God because we are members of Christ, our new birth comes through Him; it is not a new development in the order of nature but the gift of God through Jesus Christ.

When the eternal Son of God became Man in the womb of blessed Mary He took our human nature and united it with the nature of God in His own

Person. In Him we see the perfect union of the
human and divine natures which we have been trying to understand in our own case. Yet there is a
difference, and an important one; for He is the Son
of God because He Himself is God, which we are
not and cannot be, and, had He done no more than
become incarnate, the union of divine and human
nature in Him would have been a portent having
no effect of the kind of which we are thinking upon
humanity as a whole. But He did do more than
this, and His Incarnation has had a vital effect
upon humanity; for the purpose of His coming as
He did was not merely that God might become man
—though that were wonder enough—but that man
might become God. He, the Son of God by nature,
became Man that we might become the sons of God
by grace, thus He is 'first-born among many
brethren.'[1] Our sonship is derived from His, God
'hath made us accepted in the beloved,'[2] it is through
union with Him that we are the children of God.

This union with our Lord underlies all the thought
of S. Paul, he tells us that we have been 'baptized
into Christ,'[3] that we are 'in Christ,'[4] that we have
'put on Christ.'[5] That is what our Baptism means,
the putting on of the eternal Son and the abiding in
Him, or rather His taking of us into Himself.

We are sons of God because we are 'in Christ,' the
eternal Son. The love of God is so great that its
depths lie outside the comprehension of our little

[1] Rom. viii. 29.   [2] Eph. i. 6.
[3] Rom. vi. 3; Gal. iii. 27.
[4] Rom. xvi. 7; 2 Cor. v. 17; Eph. i. 3, *et al.*
[5] Gal. iii. 27.

minds and cold hearts, but this fact helps to illumin-
ate the mystery of our sonship; it is not because we
are desirable or god-like that God has adopted us,
but because of Christ Who has redeemed us, Whose
we are. In our Baptism our Lord unites us with
Himself and makes us like God through that union;
but of what kind is that union? That is the question
we have now to consider.

As on the question of sonship S. John and S. Paul
gave us two complementary conceptions of 'adoption'
and 'new birth,' through which we can at least begin
to grasp the heavenly truth, so on this question
do they give us two symbols which together form a
whole, and again S. John gives us the teaching of
our Lord. The Johannine and Pauline symbols
constantly overlap and we shall pass from the one
to the other, but we may legitimately mix symbols,
or at any rate hold them in juxtaposition, though
we may not do the like with metaphors, for a symbol
is more than a metaphor. A metaphor is illustrative
merely, and is applied to something to which it is
not literally applicable; a symbol is a description
of a spiritual fact in terms of a material one, an
epistemological necessity, and, since a spiritual truth
transcends material, two or more symbols are often
necessary to enable us to grasp it, and even then
there is something over. Let no one be alarmed,
therefore, if we find it necessary to pass from the
symbol of the vine to that of the body and back again
with a seeming indifference.

S. John gives us our Lord's teaching on our
relation to Him in the saying which I have placed
at the head of this chapter: 'I am the vine, ye are

the branches.'   Now a vine is a unity made up of
many parts; we differentiate between root, stem,
branches, leaves, flowers, and grapes, but none of
them are in the full sense separate entities, they
together make up that single plant which we call
the vine. Just so that unity which is the glorified
Christ is composed of root, stem, and branches which
bear spiritual leaves, flowers, and fruit.

To clarify this statement let us pass to the
Pauline symbol of the head and the body. This was
constantly in the mind of that great lover of S. Paul
and greatest of all Western Fathers, S. Augustine,
and it occurs over and over again in his writings;
indeed it is one of his great fundamental conceptions.
Let us take three sayings out of many, and first this :
'Christians with their Head, Who hath ascended into
heaven, are one Christ.   He is not one and we many,
but we who are many are one in that One.   Christ
therefore is one Man, the Head and the Body.'[1]   But
he goes even further. 'For Christ,' he says again,
'is not simply in the head and not in the body, but
Christ whole is in the head and in the body.'[2]   And
yet again he speaks of Christ as 'Redeeming us by
His Blood, incorporating us with Himself, making
us His own members, that in Him we also might be
Christ. . . . We all are in Him both Christ's and
Christ, since in some manner the whole Christ is
the Head and the Body.'[3]

'The whole Christ is the Head and the Body'—
that is the thought, just as the whole vine is the stem
and the branches; and the unity is so complete that

---

[1] *En. in Ps.* cxxvii. 3.   [2] *In Joan. Evang.* xxviii. 1.
[3] *En. in Ps.* xxvi. ii. 2.

the saint does not hesitate to say that 'in Him we also may be Christ,' for we all are members of that Body which is one with Him. But when we think of ourselves as members of Christ we seldom mean this, indeed the present-day connotation of the term 'member' is almost always less than this. We speak of members of a club, meaning thereby people who come together into a voluntary and accidental association for a particular purpose; the club is truly composed of its members, without whom it would not exist, and the members are the club, but their membership makes no difference to their own essential being, nor does it of itself create any underlying unity between them, and if they choose to resign their membership they are just the same men and women as they were before.

Those who look upon the Church of God primarily as an institution naturally regard it as a sort of spiritual club which may be joined or left at will without any serious consequences, and do not realize any spiritual unity either between themselves or with Christ in consequence of their membership of it; but those who understand that when we speak of the Church as the Body of Christ we are not merely indulging our taste for metaphor but enunciating a spiritual truth realize that we are members, limbs if you will, of a body, not of an association, parts of a living whole which cannot be sundered without loss and which postulates a real and not merely figurative unity of all its parts.

Christ, the second Adam, is the Head of redeemed humanity, and in Him the redeemed become one Man, He and they together because of Him.

As the branches are part of the vine so are we of
Christ, as the branches grow out of the stem so do
we grow out of Him, as the branches are one with
the stem so are we one with Him.   Union with
Christ is the present possession of every Christian
by virtue of his Baptism.   It is well to linger for a
while on this point.   We desire, those of us who
desire Christ at all, to have a more and more perfect
union with Him, and then we look at the very close
union which He vouchsafed to S. Teresa or S. John
of the Cross or to some other great saint, and it looks
as if that union is an exclusive, exalted, and mystical
thing reserved to the saints, something which we
hardly dare hope may ever be ours in this life.   But
union with Christ is not something to be attained,
not something future but something present, something which is ours here and now, not because we
are saints but because we are members of Christ's
Body.   It is true that the mystical union of the saints
differs so greatly from ours that it is hard to detect
a resemblance, but it is the difference between the
rose and the dormant 'eye,' a difference of degree
and not of kind.   In the saints that one essential
union is developed to its highest degree by the grace
of God and long years of prayer and mortification;
in us it is not so developed, but it may be, for we
have the root of the matter in us; we are not
strangers and pilgrims but fellow citizens with the
saints; we and they are equally branches of the
vine, though they are better branches.

This union with Christ is a seminal thing, a seed
capable of growth; we may overload it with all sorts
of other things, we may disregard it or sin against it,

we may make it of no, or at any rate of little, value
to us, but there it is.   Baptism can never be repeated,
its character can never be done away, because that
union with Christ once given is ours, and, if we
respond to it and tend it and grow in it as He would
have us do, it blossoms out into all the greatness and
wonder and beauty of the Christian character.   We
are called Christians because we are in Christ.

We are then branches of the vine, one with the
parent stem which is Christ and forming with Him
the whole tree, and as we have been considering this
fact there has been at the back of our minds the
realization of a further truth which becomes more
explicit in the Pauline figure of the head and the
body, namely that Christ, the Church, and ourselves
form together a spiritual organism.   The body is an
organism of which all the parts are interdependent
and mutually adjusted for the fulfilments of the ends
of its creation, and there is therefore an essential unity
between its members, all of which are formed with
a view to the rest, none of whom are ends in themselves, though each has its own individuality and its
own place in the whole.   My head may require the
use of a certain book, but it cannot get it unless my
hand takes it from the shelf, which again is impossible
if my legs do not carry me to the book-case, while
the whole operation depends upon the accurate
functioning of the entire interior economy of heart,
lungs, digestive organs, glands, and the rest, all of
which are different but mutually balanced.   Just so
with the Church there is a common unity and an
hierarchy of function in which each has its place,
so that 'if one member suffer all the members suffer

with it.'[1]   Each one of us has a place in the divine
plan within the unity of Christ's Body, a place which
no other can fill and a function which no other can
discharge, and our failure is a failure of the whole
body as our success is the success of all.   Moreover,
our fellow Christians are not merely so many people
who happen to believe approximately the same
things or attend the same church, but members of
the same body with whom it is our duty to live in
charity.   Absence of charity between the members
of a physical body is called disease, and there is no
worse disease than uncharity between Christians,
not only because it is the negation of the fundamental
Christian virtue between man and man, but also
because it destroys the very life of the Body of Christ.
The Church of Christ is an organism, not an
institution.

The vine is not only a united organism but it is an
organism which lives a common life derived from a
common source, and that source is not in the
branches but in the parent stem; just so we Christians live in the spirit not with our own life but with
the life of the parent stem which is Christ.   'I am
the vine, ye are the branches: he that abideth in
Me, and I in him, the same bringeth forth much
fruit: for without Me ye can do nothing.'

I would emphasize those last words as I think the
Lord Christ meant them to be emphasized—'Without Me ye can do nothing,' not something, but
nothing at all.   The majority of the discourage-
ments of the spiritual life arise from the fact that we
constantly think that by ourselves we can do some-

[1] 1 Cor. xii. 26, cf. whole passage, verses 12-27.

thing, though it may not be a very big something. So we set out to do that something by ourselves with the very best intentions and a good deal of hope; then we find that it does not happen, the thing is too hard for us, even though at the outset it seemed quite possible; then we forthwith become depressed, we say it is no good trying and give it all up. We should not, however, get depressed, nor should we make so many failures, if we would only realize that 'the branch *cannot* bear fruit of itself'; it is not that it does not or will not, it cannot, because it has no life in itself, all its life being derived from the tree of which it is a part: it has no independent life.

Just separate a branch from a tree and see what happens; for a time it will continue to live and look beautiful because the sap is still in it, but when the sap dries up the branch begins to wither and its flowers to disappear and in the end it is just a dead branch; you will get no fruit off a branch like that. It is just the same with ourselves, we are just branches of the vine, which is Christ, and we live with the life of the vine and no other life, and that is fundamentally what grace means to us.

Some people speak of grace as if it were a kind of dead thing, or something which can be put up into parcels and distributed, others as if it had no real existence at all. But the fact of grace is so tremendous that we can never get to the bottom of its significance; one thing we can say of it quite simply, and that is that it is the life of Christ in us. It is not just something for which we pray when we have something especially difficult to do, not something which is given at one time and withdrawn at

another, not something which comes to an end, but
it is our very life.

There is such a thing as grace given for special
purposes, and we should find it hard indeed to face
the difficulties of life without it; but the great
scholastics would never call that grace, they called
it 'a certain divine aid,' and reserved the term grace
for that even greater thing which we are now considering, the life of the parent stem which makes to
live the branches of which the vine is composed, that
life of which the Sacraments are the channels.

'I am the way and the truth,' said our Lord,
but He also said, 'I am the life,'[1] and it is that which
makes it possible for our feet to tread the way and
our minds to know the truth and by them to reach
God; and although by ourselves we can do nothing,
yet, as S. Paul reminds us, we 'can do all things
through Christ Who strengtheneth'[2] us with His own
life.

But what is it that we are to do? God expects
some result from the tremendous gifts which He
bestows, and our Lord describes this result as the
'fruit' of the divine life. 'He that abideth in Me
and I in him, the same bringeth forth much
fruit.'

God looks for fruit in us. That is the real lesson
of that acted parable of the barren fig-tree. Many
people have found difficulties in that little incident
and some have in consequence come to regard it
as a spurious addition to the Gospel story because
they could not accommodate it to the character of
Christ, but these difficulties arise from a misunder-

[1] S. John xiv. 6.   [2] Phil. iv. 13.

standing of the whole matter. Our Lord did not curse the fig-tree in a fit of childish rage or because of unsatisfied hunger. He was hungry, the tree should have borne fruit which would have satisfied that hunger, but it did not, and He cursed it so that it withered, not on account of itself but in order to impress upon the Apostles the fact that the Christian who fails to bring forth fruit is not only useless but fails to attain the end for which he has been made and redeemed, and he must consequently wither. It may seem to us an extravagant way of doing it, but when we realize the extreme difficulty with which important truths were brought home to their slow minds we cannot say it was extravagant. Rightly understood, the incident captures our imaginations so that we cannot forget it, and no doubt that is what the divine wisdom intended.

Men look, and look rightly, for fruit on the vine of the Catholic Church and oft-times they seem to find less than they would expect. That is because the branches are not bearing as they should do.

What constitutes a fruitful branch? It is one which is healthy and in which the life-giving sap has free course. If there is any disease or obstruction it may, for a time, produce leaves which give a false impression of health, but it will not bear, or if it does the fruit will be but poor. In the same way, if our souls are diseased by sin, which chokes the channels of grace, we cannot produce the fruit which our Lord would have of us. Fruit is borne on the branches of the tree, and if we, the branches, are sinful the tree of the Church cannot fulfil the purpose for which she has been planted in the

garden of the world. Sin must therefore be extir-
pated that fruit may be produced.

But what is the fruit? In detail it depends upon
the will of the Husbandman, Who is not only Husbandman but Creator and Redeemer. Every soul
is different and has its own place in the divine
economy, a place which no other can fill, but in
general the fruit is for all of us the formation of
Christ in ourselves and the fulfilment of His will in
the world around us.

How is it possible for the poor little human branch
to bring forth such divine fruit? It is so difficult to
be like Christ and to keep to His will, and we are
so weak. Let us go a step further, a big step further
but a necessary one, and say that we are nothing,
that we cannot bear this fruit. That is the plain
truth, and at first sight it seems to cut the ground
completely from under us. It seems that if we are
nothing and can do nothing we had better give up
the whole matter at once and relapse into futile
pessimism.

That is the first thought, but like so many first
thoughts it is the wrong one, the true conclusion is
the exact opposite. Truly we are nothing and can
do nothing, but we are in Christ Who fills us with
His life; we can therefore do everything that He
wills us to do. He knows that we by ourselves can
bring forth nothing at all, but He also knows that
by the life which He pours into us we can indeed
bring forth the fruit which He desires to see; it is
His fruit and not ours. So the parent stem of the
vine realizes Himself in us; He brings forth in us
the fruit which He would have, but He can only do

so if we consciously, deliberately, and intentionally abide in Him.

'Abide in Me, and I in you. . . . If a man abide not in Me, he is cast forth as a branch, and is withered; and men gather them, and cast them into the fire, and they are burned.'[1]   Naturally, because they are only branches, dead wood. 'Abide in Me,' that is our Lord's word to us. The symbol of the vine breaks down here (as all symbols must at some point since the material can never wholly explain the spiritual), and we pass from the vegetable to the volitional sphere. The branch of the vine has no choice, either it abides in the vine or it gets broken or cut off; but it is not so with us, we have our wills, we may cling closely to the Lord Christ or we may let Him go, we may give His life free course in our hearts or we may become severed from that life by our own volition.

What then? The whole possibility of perfection, of the divine will realizing itself in our persons, depends upon the generous simplicity of our own wills, not upon their strength but upon their goodness. We can give ourselves to the fullness of divine life or we can commit spiritual suicide; for the grace of God waits upon our own response. We must be content to abide in Him and let Him produce His fruit in us with our co-operation, for it is His fruit, our virtues are His, our successes His, our joy His. It is a wonderful thing to be the branch of Christ.

[1] S. John xv. 4, 6.

CHAPTER III

TEMPLES OF THE HOLY GHOST

'*Know ye not that ye are the temple of God, and that the Spirit of God dwelleth in you?*'—1 COR. iii. 16.

WE have been trying to understand something of that new order of creation into which God lifts us in Baptism, that newness which is ours in Christ; we have found in it a new status, in that we are no longer merely the creatures of God but His sons; new being, resulting from that birth from above and from our union with the eternal Son; new life, flowing from that relationship to God.

In all this we are related to the transcendent Father and to the heavenly Christ into Whose being we are subsumed that, in the awe-inspiring thought of S. Augustine, we may become Him. But our relationship is not only with the transcendent God but also with God immanent; if God takes us into Himself He also enters into us by the Holy Spirit, and it is that Spirit of Whom we now need to think.

There are two levels of human life in the world; S. Paul calls them 'flesh' and 'spirit,' they may also be called 'the natural' and 'the supernatural.' S. Paul does not mean by 'the flesh' merely absorption in carnal desires, though that may well be its most extreme form; he means the predominance of the lower self which is characteristic of fallen

humanity unassisted by divine grace. God does as
a matter of fact in particular cases raise fallen
humanity to great heights apart from the grace of
the Church, the 'flesh' is not always fleshly: but it
cannot attain to that intimacy with Him which is
His gift to His sons. That is supernatural and per-
tains to what S. Paul calls 'spirit'; it is characteristic
not of man alone but of man indwelt by the Holy
Spirit, and it is that indwelling which is, according
to the Apostle, the mark of the Christian. 'If any
man have not the Spirit of Christ,' he tells us, 'he
is none of His.'[1] This indwelling of the Spirit,
S. John says, 'the world cannot receive, because
it seeth Him not, neither knoweth Him: but ye
know Him; for He dwelleth with you, and shall be
in you.'[2]

The Church, then, is not only the Body of Christ,
but being that Body she is the spiritual organism in
which the Holy Spirit is immanent and energizing
in the world; the spirit-bearing Body. The human
body lives because it is indwelt by the spirit of man,
even so the Body of Christ lives because it is indwelt
by the Spirit of Christ. Christ did not leave behind
Him a living Church when He ascended into heaven.
He left a Body prepared for life, a life into which it
entered when the Holy Spirit came upon it at
Pentecost; so Pentecost, and not an earlier date, is
the birthday of the Church.

In His last discourse our Lord uses three words
concerning the Holy Spirit which we must examine;
and the first of these is *send*. He speaks of 'the
Comforter, which is the Holy Ghost, Whom the

[1] Rom. viii. 9.   [2] S. John xiv. 17.

Father will send in My Name,'[1] and twice over of
'the Comforter Whom I will send unto you.'[2]   The
Holy Ghost, Who is Himself God, is sent by the
Father and the Son.

There was a former sending of God when the
Father sent the Son into the world at the Incarnation; that was a coming of the eternal Son in the
flesh to reveal God and save mankind, so at Pentecost there was another coming of God, this time of
the Holy Spirit, and for another purpose, to direct,
strengthen, and sanctify saved humanity.

Let us realize that it is God Who came at Pentecost and God Who comes to us. When we think
of the operations of the divine Persons it is very easy
to fall into tritheism, and to very many people the
Son is not only a different Person but a different
God from the Father, and the Holy Ghost different
from both; but there is no distinction in essence
between the three Persons, we believe and must
believe in one God; our difficulty arises from having
to describe a divine and (in the right sense) incomprehensible mystery in human language.   The Holy
Spirit is not another or an inferior God, He *is* God
Who came upon the Church and enters into us.

Further, He is God and not a created gift or
emanation. We speak so easily of a spirit of love
or peace or joy, and of the spirit of a great teacher
living in his followers, that it is easy, too easy, to
think of the Holy Spirit as nothing more than a
mental disposition or an influence of God.   But God
gives us more than that in holy Church; He comes
Himself to be in us.

[1] S. John xiv. 26.   [2] ibid., xv. 26; xvi. 7.

The second word of which we must think is *give*. 'I will pray the Father,' said our Lord, 'and He shall give you another Comforter.'[1] This takes our minds back to what we have just said, 'Another Comforter'; Jesus Himself was the first Comforter, Who came by the will of the Father to reveal and save; the Holy Spirit is the second Comforter, Who comes again by the will of the Father to guide our minds in regard to that revelation, to show us the will of God, to strengthen and sanctify those whom the Son saves. But it is not only a coming of which we are thinking but a giving; in the coming of the Holy Spirit God gives Himself into our hearts to be a present, something which is our very own. God in His infinite humility gives Himself to us for our use and enjoyment. Just as in the Blessed Sacrament Jesus gives us Himself as the food of our souls, so in Baptism and Confirmation does the Holy Spirit give us Himself, and that gift He never takes away; the Holy Spirit is always in us, though we seldom realize it as we should.

And the third word is *abide*. 'He shall give you another Comforter, that He may abide with you for ever.'[2] We have remarked that the Holy Spirit never removes the gift of Himself which is once made, but this word 'abide' means more than that, as our Lord says again, 'He dwelleth with you and shall be in you.'[3] He comes not only to be with us, but to abide, to dwell within the soul. This is a thought upon which we may well linger.

'In the beginning,' we read in the first words of

[1] ibid., xiv. 16.   [2] ibid., xiv. 16.
[3] ibid., xiv. 17.

the Bible, 'God created the heaven and the earth.
And the earth was without form, and void; and
darkness was upon the face of the deep. And the
Spirit of God moved upon the face of the waters.'¹
So we see the Holy Spirit present in the forming
world, moving, energizing, bringing the ordered creation out of the formlessness and darkness of the deep;
in the Old Testament we see Him moving and
inspiring the prophets, leading Israel up to God,
and in mankind generally we find many evidences
of His beneficent presence, for God is immanent in
all things, and more especially in the minds of men,
by the Holy Spirit, 'the Lord and giver of life.'
What, then, are we to say of His presence in us?
Is it, can it be, anything more than this?

There is a real and great difference between the
Spirit's presence in the world and His indwelling of
the Body of Christ. Our Lord speaks of Him as
'the Spirit of truth; Whom the world cannot receive,'² but He comes to us as a gift to be received,
a Person Who is not only present with and working
in us but Who indwells us, God to be known and
worshipped. All these three words which we have
been considering bring home to us the fact that the
Holy Spirit's presence with us is a much greater
thing than His presence in creation generally;
He is present with us in a new and more fundamental way.

We must, however, not exaggerate the character
of the divine indwelling. He does not take the place
of the human spirit in us as in the hypostatic union
of the eternal Son with the sacred humanity of Jesus,

¹ Gen. i. 1-2.   ² S. John xiv. 17.

nor does He inspire us with a private and plenary inspiration so that all our ideas and movements are from Him; He is God and we are still human. It is necessary to remind ourselves of this because many people when they believe a particular course of action to be right are equally sure that that and nothing else is the will of God made clear to them by the inspiration of the Holy Ghost, whereas it may be nothing more than their own self-will. The movement of the indwelling Spirit is not by way of plenary inspiration and an automatic control of the human spirit, we still have our own minds which may make mistakes and our own wills with which we may make the wrong choice. The Holy Spirit directs, strengthens, and sanctifies us, but He does not abrogate any part of our humanity.

What, then, is the office of the Holy Spirit in the Christian soul? We have already thought of Him as the moving power, the personal immanent agent of the creative act of God, and what is true of the natural creation is also true of the supernatural, for He is the agent of the new creation.

Our Lord speaks of the new birth of Baptism as being 'of water and of the Spirit,'[1] and S. Paul speaks of 'the Spirit of adoption.'[2] His ministry in us is not by way of substitution but of development; it is He through Whom the new life is given and comes to perfection. The new creation is superimposed upon material of the old order which has to be disciplined and made amenable to God and does not attain to perfection all at once. Obviously the perfecting of our nature is far beyond us even with the aid of

[1] ibid., iii. 5.   [2] Rom. viii. 15.

grace, it requires the action of God immanent in us; so it is the Holy Spirit Who gradually transforms the natural man into the supernatural, Who brings the material of the old order under the transforming influence of the new and develops the character of Christ in us.

His action is very quiet, very secret, and, be it said, very ordinary. There are those who expect that the action of the Holy Spirit should be by the extraordinary, the unexpected, by cutting clean across the common ways of life. There are, of course, extraordinary movements of the Spirit to deal with extraordinary circumstances, but not wantonly extraordinary ones, such as would make for disorder, for chaos rather than cosmos; rather is the Holy Spirit the spirit of order, the still small voice, and those who look for Him in the fire and the whirl-wind are likely to be deceived.

The Holy Spirit is God present in us. His presence, then, is that of a Person, not an influence, and our relationship to Him is personal. We seldom realize that God is within us in this way because it is hard to visualize the personality of the Holy Spirit, yet none but a person can dwell in anything. An influence may be present but only a person can indwell. If this were more fully realized our relationship with Him would be more of a reality than it generally is; for the most part He can do so little with us because we do not understand that He is there; yet He is there as God within His temple.

'Know ye not that ye are the temple of God, and that the Spirit of God dwelleth in you?' It would seem as though a great number of Christians did not know this, for they take but little notice of the indwelling Spirit. Yet a temple exists for the habitation of God and the worshippers' business is wholly with Him. It would seem as though we were in danger of making ourselves something quite other than the temple of God.

We need, then, to respond to the Holy Spirit within us. His control over us, as we have seen, is not automatic; as in all things, God respects the freedom of will which He has given us and will in no wise overrule our action, and thus it is that the work of our sanctification has two sides, the movement of the Spirit and our own response. If we do not respond, the Holy Spirit will not force us to perfection; and S. Paul has warned us that we can grieve, resist, and even quench Him. How, then, may we, His temples, respond to His indwelling that He may perfect the new creation of God in us? By going out to Him in faith that He may enlighten the darkness of our minds, by lifting ourselves to Him in love that He may warm the coldness of our hearts, and by generous worship that He may form Christ in us.

CHAPTER IV

THE BREAD OF LIFE

'*I am the Bread of Life. . . . As the living Father hath sent Me, and I live by the Father: so he that eateth Me, even he shall live by Me.*'—S. JOHN vi. 35, 57.

WE have to consider in this chapter the mystery of Jesus in the Blessed Sacrament. It is manifestly impossible within the limits of a single chapter to consider it in its completeness, nor shall we attempt to do so. What we shall try to think about is Jesus as the Bread of Life.

The offering of the Mass is essentially a godward action, our Lord is present primarily as Priest and Victim to plead His Sacrifice for us; it is thus that the Mass is a 'remembrance' of Him which He commands us to 'do.' He is also present that we may worship Him with intimate, loving reverence. But it is for neither of these purposes that He comes in the precise manner that He does come.

It is a wonderful thing that the eternal Son of God chooses to be present on our altars under the forms of bread and wine, a fact so striking that we are compelled to ask why it is. That He should 'empty Himself of His glory' and come into this world as a man, that He should accept the conditions of our humanity and live and suffer and die as a man, that He should accept not worship but ignominy and

death from His creatures is wonder enough; but that
He should give Himself into the hands of men in the
humble, domestic forms of bread and wine is far
more so.   The sacrifice of the Mass could have been
performed, had it been the divine will, without the
acceptance of this lowly guise, He could have made
Himself available to our worship without it.   Why,
then, does He choose these humble necessities of
our bodily life in which to veil His glorious presence?
There is but one answer, because He comes to be
His people's food.   He comes as bread that we may
eat Him, as wine that we may drink Him, that in
His Sacrament we may feed upon Him.   Let us
realize that fact in all its startling simplicity: 'I am
the Bread of Life,' the food of My people, thus to
supply their most elementary need.

Every living thing in the world has need of food
to sustain and develop the life that is in it for its own
growth and perfection, and that food is right for it
which supplies just what it needs for these purposes;
if it cannot get that food it wastes and dies.   Some
animals live on seeds, some on nuts, others on grass,
and others again on flesh of some kind, each according to his needs; a cow could not sustain life on the
food proper to a dog, and so in the ordered plan of
nature each animal finds and uses the food proper
to its own nature.   So too man lives on the food
proper to him, but he has wider needs than the
animals, not only does his body require food but
his mind and his soul also, and without their nourish-
ment the mind and soul, no less than the body, grow
weak and stunted and die.

Spiritual food is therefore necessary to sustain life,

and that divine life which is given to us in Baptism
requires its own food if it is to be sustained and
developed, which food, since we live with His life,
can be nothing less than Christ Himself.   It is clear,
then, that the Blessed Sacrament is not accidental
to Christian life but necessary to it, not of its *bene
esse* but of its *esse*.   A form of Christianity which
ignores the Bread of Life is stunted.   Custom has
produced amongst us a type of popular religion
which is frankly non-sacramental.   In many, perhaps
most, country parishes the reception of Holy Communion is not merely infrequent among the bulk of
the population but non-existent; this is more than
unfortunate, it is a cutting off of life at its source.
Non-communicant Christians have indeed received
the life of Christ through their union with Him in
Baptism, but they are not nourished by the food
which is necessary to the continuance of that life
and are consequently living on a sub-Christian basis.
The fault is in most cases not theirs, it results from
ignorance of the nature and necessity of the Blessed
Sacrament, and in persons of real piety God does
make up for the loss by feeding their souls in other
ways, not infrequently producing beautiful Christian
characters; nevertheless, the loss is there, an essential
element of Christian life is lacking.

If Christ is the food of the Christian it is clear that
He intends His Sacrament for all and not for some;
He is *esca viatorum* not *sanctorum*, the food of all His
children who desire to follow Him in their pilgrim-
age to the heavenly Jerusalem, not only of saints.
The occasionally heard objection of the non-
communicant that he is not good enough to receive

our Lord therefore falls to the ground, not because
nobody is good enough, though that is of course
true, but because the Blessed Sacrament is intended
for our food and not for our reward.   If a man has
fallen into mortal sin he needs the cleansing of
absolution before he can rightly approach the most
Holy, but he needs the most Holy that he may rise
above his temptations into newness of life.   He needs
that food all the more because he is weak, that by
it he may be made strong.

Christ is the efficient cause of our spiritual life,
He gives life and His own life to our souls, that much
has been made clear already; but not only does He
give us life, He also sustains and develops that life,
and as we receive it by entering into a particular
relationship to Him so He sustains and develops it
in us by entering into a further relationship to us,
by giving Himself to be our food; 'he that eateth
Me, even he shall live by Me.'[1]

Natural food contains those principles which are
necessary to the continuance and building up of our
bodily life, which principles by the process of digestion penetrate into our whole body, there being no
part of us which is not nourished thereby, so without
our being conscious of it every meal that we take
affects the whole of our body.   In the same way the
Blessed Sacrament permeates our whole soul, building it up and filling it with life, though we may not
be conscious that this process is going on.   The
benefit of Holy Communion does not reside in its
affective fervent reception but in our goodwill, our
readiness, our desire to feed upon our Lord; some-

[1] S. John vi. 57.

times He gives us to realize something of the power of His coming, just as sometimes we know certainly that our bodily food has done us good, and often, more often, He does not; but the power is there whether we feel it or not, permeating our soul, building up its every tissue and renewing in us the life of Christ.

And here we ask ourselves again the question, Why does our Lord come to us in bread and wine? Why are these material things necessary to His gift? And the answer is, Because He comes to be the food of the whole man.

When He became incarnate our Lord took to Himself not our soul alone but our whole being, that He might save and sanctify not part of us only but all our selves. In this life we are made up of soul and body which, while they are separable in thought, form together a unity which can be broken only by death, and it is that composite being which is the man that Christ came to save. So as He once came in the flesh our Lord comes in the Sacrament united with a material form that He may give life not to our souls alone but to our bodies as well, that He may unite Himself with our souls and bodies, giving Himself to our whole being in the most radical way possible. The material part of the Sacrament is then something far more than a convenient outward sign by which we may be assured that we have received a spiritual benefit, it is the means whereby our Lord gives Himself to our whole being, so, in giving the Blessed Sacrament to the communicant, the Church requires the priest to say to him: 'The Body of our Lord Jesus

Christ, which was given for thee, preserve thy body and soul unto everlasting life.' So is He the food of the whole man.

In taking the food of the body we transform it into ourselves, but the food of the soul produces an exactly contrary effect, for it transforms us into Christ. S. Leo says that 'the participation in the Body and Blood of Christ has no other effect than to transform us into that which we receive,'[1] and S. Augustine speaks of our Lord's saying to him, 'Thou shalt not convert Me like common food into thy substance, but thou shalt be changed into Me.'[2] When we make our Communion we receive the whole Christ, His Body and Blood, His soul, His humanity, His divinity into our whole selves, soul and body; we receive far more than a created gift, we receive Him, and, He being what He is, the effect of that reception must be the changing of our soul into Him, startling though that statement seems to be. The change is not instantaneous, it suffers many set-backs from our own weakness and sinfulness, but a change it is, and as we go on making our Communions it becomes more and more radical and complete. It is never perfect in this life, for we do not reach absolute perfection in anything this side of heaven, but it is real and becomes progressively deeper; gradually, as we are able to bear it, we are transformed into that which we receive.

But the analogy must be pressed a stage further. We may partake of the most wholesome and nourishing meal, but if our digestion is impaired we shall not receive the benefit of it; likewise if our spiritual

[1] *Serm. de Pass. LXIII*, xii. 7.   [2] *Conf.* vii. 10.

digestion is sick we shall indeed partake of Christ,
but we shall not be transformed into Him. Our
Lord does not ask of us great virtue when we come
to receive Him, for He comes to bring forth His
virtues in us; but He does require the two first
requisites of spiritual health: simple faith and sin-
cere penitence. By faith we place ourselves simply
and wholly in His hands for Him to do in us what
He will, and by penitence we disengage ourselves
from our sinful tendencies and seek His pardon for
sin done. If these are present the divine food
cannot fail of its effect.

Our Lord gives Himself to us in the Blessed
Sacrament and transforms us into Himself, and
uniting Himself with us in an ineffable manner He
gives us union with Himself. In the depths of our
being we are already united with Him by Baptism,
but this union is by way of personal intimacy. We
have considered the Blessed Sacrament as the food
of our souls and so it is, but that food is no created
gift but Christ Himself; it is a Person Who nourishes
us with Himself, it is a Person Who embraces us,
and we are united with Him as persons. So the
union of the Blessed Sacrament is a personal relationship. But see how close it is. It is possible for
two human beings to be very closely united with
each other, so closely that they seem to know each
other's unspoken thoughts, the union of holy
marriage has been compared by the Apostle to that
which is between Christ and His Church; but the
union between Christ and the soul in the Blessed
Sacrament is closer than these. Men and women,
however deep and wonderful their union with each

other may be, still remain fundamentally separate, their personalities touch but cannot mingle; but Christ transforms the soul into Himself so that it is fundamentally one with Him, so that it lives not with its own separate life but with His. He is not only its friend and lover but the food which maintains its very life. Words fail to express the depth of this personal union, experience can only tell us something of what in its perfection it is.

'He that eateth My Flesh, and drinketh My Blood, dwelleth in Me, and I in him.'[1] Christ dwells in the soul and it in Him in the sweet intimacy of personal union. The effect then of Holy Communion is not transitory. Our Lord in His love comes to us again and again in the Blessed Sacrament, as often as we will. Each visit is a new one and may be said, from our point of view at any rate, to come to an end, but its effects continue. Christ does not leave us, each Communion does but deepen the divine indwelling, of which we cannot properly speak in terms of time. To return to our original thought; a meal comes to an end when we have taken our food, but the food is in us and remains building up our body even after the digestive process has come to an end. Even so Christ comes to us and we receive Him and go out into the world again, but He is still dwelling in us, building up the soul and bringing forth His virtues in it, and we may still have sweet converse with Him in our hearts.

The eternal Son became incarnate in the flesh to accomplish the will of the Father in regard to mankind, and that will is still accomplished by incarna-

[1] S. John vi. 56.

D

tion; the principle is the same though the mode is different. In His Body, the Church, Christ is incarnate until the end of time, through her and in her He reconciles men to God, giving them life and light to fulfil the purpose which God has for them. In our Baptism we become part of that Body; but in Holy Communion Christ becomes incarnate once more in us as individual Christians; He, God and man, goes forth in our persons to accomplish in the world that which the Father wills us to accomplish for Him, so that we are each one of us Christophers bearing Him Who is the Life, the Light, the Salvation of the world. It is a sobering thought, and one which should fill us with the deepest humility and penitence. Christ gives Himself to us not merely that we may enjoy Him but that through us He may save the world; through us, that is, not only as members of the saving organism of His Church, but also as individuals. We have an individual responsibility to Him in this matter as persons in whom He dwells.

In the world to-day individuality counts for less than it has probably ever done in the history of civilization, and there is a real danger that it may be unduly minimized in the Church also. We are rightly being recalled to a sense of our responsibility to the whole Body of Christ, a responsibility which has too often and too widely been lost sight of, but there is a danger that in this recall it may be forgotten that that responsibility is one which is discharged by individuals; that if Christ dwells in the Church, as He most certainly does, He also dwells in each man, woman, and child who belongs

to that Church, and He cannot save the world completely through the Church unless He is doing it
through every individual who composes it. The
value of each soul is incalculable not because man
is, as used to be said, the crown of creation, but
because God loves each one of us personally and
because He makes us agents of His Son Who gives
Himself to us in the Blessed Sacrament that He may
save the world through us.

If this is so, no Christian has any right to be
content with his own sinfulness and mediocrity. If
we realize the whole wonder of our vocation, we shall
seek to give ourselves, humbly, penitently, and
generously, to our Lord Who gives Himself so
perfectly to us; we shall desire to be wholly and not
only partly filled with Him. This demands self-
discipline (of which we are not now thinking) and
a regular approach to the Blessed Sacrament.

The Church requires that we make our Communion at least three times a year, but no devout
Christian could possibly be content with that. It
is customary to instruct Confirmation candidates to
receive our Lord once a month, which is better
but still not ideal. Our Lord, on the other hand,
teaches us to pray, 'Give us this day our daily bread,'
and it is at least arguable that He has in mind here
not merely natural bread for our bodies but also
supernatural bread for our souls.

It is impossible to lay down a general rule in such
a matter, but it is hardly too optimistic to believe
that daily, or almost daily, Communion could be
much more general than in fact it is; there are many
devout souls who could and should receive our Lord

as frequently as this who yet hold back from doing
so. Motives vary, sometimes they are right, sometimes mistaken, but it may be legitimate to suggest
that the question which we put to ourselves on this
matter should not be, 'Why should I make my
Communion every day?' but, 'Why should I *not* do
so?'

Whatever the individual answer to this question
may be, one thing is clear, namely, that no serious
Christian should regard a Sunday as well kept upon
which he has not received his Lord. 'The Lord's
Service on the Lord's Day' is a good maxim, but
it is far too widely considered that it is quite enough
to hear Mass on Sunday and to make one's Communion once a month or even less often. The
practice of the early Church seems to have been not
only weekly Mass but weekly Communion, and it
is a practice to which we shall do well to return.

In saying this we must not be understood to con-
demn, as is being widely done to-day, the custom
which has become very widespread of receiving Holy
Communion at an early Mass and attending a later
one for devotion. Contrary to the latest trend of
opinion, we would maintain that there is much to
be said for this habit. The human mind is so
constructed that it cannot easily focus itself upon
two things at once; but the Mass is two things, or
rather has two aspects, Sacrifice and Communion,
and it is a real devotional gain to many to be able,
after making their Communion earlier in the day, to
concentrate on the sacrificial and intercessory aspect
of the Mass later on. The ideal of the Parish Mass
at which every one makes his or her Communion

is a fine one and one for which there is much to be said; but there is more to be said on the other side than is often allowed, and those who find the other custom to be more devotionally fruitful to themselves must not on that account be labelled as individualists, nor should the custom of hearing Mass without communicating be frowned upon.

'I am the Bread of Life. . . . As the living Father hath sent Me, and I live by the Father: so he that eateth Me, even he shall live by Me.' As we learn to live upon the Sacrament, not merely occasionally receive it, we shall find ourselves, almost unconsciously, living by Him Who is the Sacrament; and as we live by Him He will change us more and more perfectly into His likeness and accomplish His will in and through us by that deep personal union with Himself which is His greatest gift to sinful man.

CHAPTER V

FAITH

'*Then came the disciples to Jesus apart, and said, Why could not we cast him out? And Jesus said unto them, Because of your unbelief.*'—S. MATT. xvii. 19-20.

WHEN our Lord and the three disciples came down from the Mount of Transfiguration they found a great bother going on at the bottom. A man had brought his lunatic son to the other disciples to be cured, and they had done all that they could, but the cure had not taken place; the boy was just as bad as ever. So the distracted father brought him to Jesus and He healed him at once. But the disciples were very worried at their own failure. 'Why,' they said, 'why could not we cast him out?'

It is easy for us to think of excuses for them. The boy may have been a particularly bad case or the devil unusually powerful, indeed our Lord tells them that 'This kind can come forth by nothing but by prayer and fasting.'[1] After all, our Lord was God and they but men, is it so very surprising that they failed in an enterprise which evidently required the divine power to bring it to a successful issue?

However much we may desire to be kind to them, the fact remains that they knew they had failed our

[1] Verse 21.

Lord, and He knew it.   The healing of the sick and
the casting out of devils are certainly impossible to
the natural man, but the point to remember in this
case is that the disciples were not just natural men,
they were men whom our Lord had chosen and to
whom He had given power to do, among other
things, exactly this which they had failed to do. For
we are told in an earlier chapter that 'when He had
called unto Him His twelve disciples, He gave them
power against unclean spirits, to cast them out,
and to heal all manner of sickness and all manner
of disease. . . . These twelve Jesus sent forth, and
commanded them, saying, . . . preach, . . . heal
the sick, cleanse the lepers, raise the dead, cast out
devils.'[1]   They had been given a power which was
not their own, just as we are given grace which is
not our own, and when the need to exercise it arose
they were unable to meet it; they failed in the very
thing for which they were sent, the very purpose for
which power had been given to them.   There had
been a failure then and a remarkable one, and the
question which we have to investigate is, Where does
the cause of that failure lie?

The divine power was a reality, and it was truly
given, but apparently it was possible for that power
to fail, to be as though it were not, which is a very
serious matter.   It was so even for our Lord Himself,
for we are told that in certain environments even
He was unable to do any mighty works.

If this is true of the special power given to the
disciples and the like power of our Lord, it is also
true of the grace which He gives us in the Church.

[1] S. Matt. x. 1, 5, 7, 8.

There has been much controversy as to the irre-sistibility of grace which resolves itself into the question whether grace can fail or not. Whatever our theological views on this matter, it seems clear in practice that grace can fail. We have seen it fail in the Apostles, in countless Christians, and in ourselves.

But to what are we to attribute this failure? It can hardly be in grace itself, which, since it is the power of God, must be indefectible, for God cannot fail; the failure must lie in its effects, there must be something faulty in its connection with the human agent.

God Who has created us always respects the integrity of the nature which He has given, and will by no means overrule our freedom or take away from what is proper to our personality. According to the full theory of irresistible grace the Christian is no more than an automaton, set in motion by God, and without any power to resist or deflect the divine movement. In spite of its patent falsity such a theory is by no means uncommon, but it degrades human nature and ascribes failure to God Who cannot fail, rather than to man who, without God, could do little else.

Grace brings forth its fruits in and through the human agent and for its success it demands a certain attitude of mind and heart; when it fails it does so not because it is weak in itself but because of the absence of the right kind of response. This is clear from our Lord's teaching, for, when the disciples asked Him, 'Why could not we cast him out?' He did not answer, 'Because My grace was insufficient

for you,' but, 'Because of your unbelief.' It is human
unbelief, then, which is the cause of the failure of
divine grace and not any defect in the grace itself.

But this word 'unbelief' in its ordinary meaning
conveys a wrong impression of what was in our Lord's
mind. He could hardly convict the disciples of
unbelief and hardness of heart, they did believe in
Him. As it stands the word is a mistranslation,
what He said was not *unbelief* in the sense of having
no faith at all, but *little faith*; they had some faith
but it was insufficient.

It is clear, then, that while we may possess the
fullness of the divine gift it is necessary for us to
appropriate it by a very definite faith before it can
become operative in us; it must become part of us
and the ruling principle of our lives if it is to bear
fruit, and it can only do so by our own act of faith.
We can by our lack of faith render it inoperative.
The gift is there, faith does not create but accepts it.

Faith, then, is the fundamental response of the
Christian to the grace which is his, 'as many as
received Him, to them gave He power to become
the sons of God, even to them that believe on His
Name.'[1]

S. Paul tells us that we are 'justified by faith' and
'are all the children of God by faith in Christ Jesus,'[2]
and in saying this he does not mean us to infer that
our faith is the cause of our justification and new
birth, but that it is the means whereby these gifts
have free course in us and make us what God would
have us be.

This point is illustrated over and over again by

[1] S. John i. 12.   [2] Gal. iii. 24, 26.

our Lord's miracles. The power to heal was not
in those who were healed, it was in our Lord, they
were the recipients of it; nevertheless they could not
receive the benefits of the divine power unless they
themselves had faith not in it but in Him. Thus in
the incident of the blind men our Lord asked them
before He did anything, 'Believe ye that I am able
to do this? They said unto Him, Yea, Lord. Then
touched He their eyes, saying, According to your
faith be it unto you.'[1] In the case of the Syro-
phoenician woman He 'answered and said unto her,
O woman, great is thy faith: be it unto thee even
as thou wilt. And her daughter was made whole
from that very hour.'[2] In the case of the woman
with the issue of blood virtue seems to have been
drawn from our Lord by the touch of faith even
without His own volition, and the story has an interest
all its own from that circumstance. 'Jesus, imme-
diately knowing in Himself that virtue had gone out
of Him, turned Him about in the press, and said,
Who touched My clothes? . . . And He said unto
her, Daughter, thy faith hath made thee whole; go
in peace, and be whole of thy plague.'[3]

We might multiply examples indefinitely, but
these are sufficient for our purpose, proving as they
do the necessity of faith to the operation of the divine
power; and that this is true not only in the extraordinary exercise of that power in miracle but also
in the ordinary outpouring of power in our salvation
is clear from our Lord's words to Nicodemus, 'God
so loved the world, that He gave His only-begotten

[1] S. Matt. ix. 28, 29.   [2] ibid., xv. 28.
[3] S. Mark v. 30, 34.

Son, that whosoever believeth in Him should not
perish, but have everlasting life.'[1]   Our very
salvation depends on faith in our Lord Jesus
Christ.

We begin, then, with the confession of S. Peter,
'Thou art the Christ, the Son of the living God.'[2]
This was the perfect expression of the Apostle's faith
and it is the ground of ours, faith in the divinity of
our Lord and in the Father through Him.   Faith
not in this or that fact about our Lord, but in Him.
We do believe in certain facts about Him, His
Incarnation, Crucifixion, Resurrection, and Ascension, all that we are told about Him in the Gospel,
but these are all ancillary to our faith in Himself,
it is in Him that we believe essentially and in Him
as God.   Those theories which detract from the
divinity of Jesus cut at the root of all God's gifts in
Him; if He be not God, little reliance can be placed
upon His revelation of the Father; if He be not
God, there can be no grace such as we have been
considering.   It is because He is God that the Father
reveals Himself in Him and makes men His sons
through Him; it is because He is God that we can
be saved.   We must guard our faith in that holy
mystery most jealously.   'Faith in the divinity of
Jesus is, according to the designs of the Father, the
first thing needful in order to share in the divine
life.'[3]

But of what kind is our faith to be?   It is obvious
that certain kinds are insufficient; for the disciples,
as we have seen, were not totally deficient in faith,

---

[1] S. John iii. 16.   [2] S. Matt. xvi. 16.
[3] Marmion, *Christ the Life of the Soul*, p. 129.

but what they had did not prevent them from failing
our Lord when put to the test.

Faith begins on the intellectual level as an assent
to facts, it is based upon reasoning and yet it is more
than logical thought because it does not proceed
from proved premises to equally proved conclusions,
but accepts facts which transcend logical proof
because it believes them to be consonant with
reason.   When we attain to this sort of faith we have
made the first step towards God, and it is a big one;
nevertheless, we have not yet arrived at perfect faith,
we are still elementary.

The second step is a bigger one still, from the
intellectual to the spiritual, from assent to conviction.
It is not merely thought but apprehension.   As
S. Augustine says, 'Faith is the first principle which
subdues the soul to God; then the precepts of life.
When these are guarded hope is strengthened and
charity nourished, and that which previously was
but belief begins to be light.'[1]

This kind of faith marks the transition from belief
to light, it is less an intellectual act (though the
intellect still has its part in it) than a spiritual
illumination, and the truth believed becomes as it
were part of ourselves.   There are moments in the
lives of us all when a truth hitherto obscure and
perhaps apparently unimportant suddenly shines out
with a sort of radiance, we see it and know it with a
sense of discovery and it becomes our own, a conviction which we are henceforward quite sure about
and which is consequently unshakable.

But ultimately faith has to do not with truths but

[1] *de Agone Christiano*, xiii. 14.

with Truth.   The mysteries which faith makes real
to us are not discoverable by human effort, they are
revealed by God, and the ultimate act of faith is not
in them but in Him.   When our Lord said to the
blind men, 'Believe ye that I am able to do this?'
He was fixing their attention not upon the act of
healing but upon Himself, the emphasis is on the
personal pronoun.   He was able because He was
God and, however dim their perception of His
Person may have been, the reply of the blind men
was an act of faith in that Person.   So, then, faith
is in its essence an attitude of soul towards a person.
This comes out very clearly in the conversation at
the foot of the Mount of Transfiguration.   The faith
which our Lord there said was the condition of the
disciples' working the works of Christ was a personal
thing, an attitude of soul towards Himself, forming
a spiritual link between Him and them so that
when that link became loosened the power departed.

Faith in Christ is a complete trust in Him because
He is what He is; because of what we know of
Him we believe in Him as God and trust Him
as God, not merely the unknown God but God
revealed in man.   Such faith does not demand
intellectual demonstration, it is content to leave
many things unexplained.   Our Lord does not give
us a complete answer to every question which the
human mind can devise, nor did He intend to do
so; He shows us Himself and what is necessary for
us to live by (what S. Augustine in the passage
quoted above calls *praecepta vivendi*) and He asks us
to trust His word because He is the Word of God.
In that trust is the faith which makes God and Christ

and all the wonders of grace our very own.   Because
we trust in Him we believe His word and enter into
the experience of His power.

This is quite reasonable, although it so far transcends reason.   We have faith in our fellow man if
we know him thoroughly and find him to be upright
and honourable, and having that faith in him we
accept what he says without asking him to prove his
every word.   Indeed, the more we trust him the less
we desire such proof, and our faith in him brings
such a knowledge of him as we could not have
otherwise.   It is the same with regard to God.   He
is the eternal Truth, and if we put our trust in Him
we shall certainly not be deceived, rather shall we
enter into a real knowledge of Him and a relation
deeper than any human friendship.

By faith we embrace God in all the plenitude of
His Being, we find Him and know Him; this leads
us from trust to confidence, from trust in Himself we
proceed to confidence in His goodwill, so faith goes
hand in hand with the allied virtue of hope, for 'faith
is the substance of things hoped for, the evidence of
things not seen.'[1]   The Christian should be no easy
optimist, nevertheless he cannot be an ultimate
pessimist; because he believes in God he knows that
the motive of creation is love, and that in spite of all
the evil that is in the world through sin and all the
pain and suffering which is entwined with our life
on earth, God's purpose is the perfect good and
eternal happiness of His people; so through the
certainty of faith he comes to a sure and certain hope
in the goodwill of God Who is his Father.   Hope

[1] Heb. xi. 1.

is a sure confidence in the purpose of Almighty God;
confidence in God Himself not only as our first cause
but also as our final end and our eternal beatitude.
Believing that God has made us for Himself, hope
points to heaven not as a vague possibility but as the
end to which, if we are faithful, God purposes to
bring us because that is the end of our creation.
However much His will may be resisted and
obstructed by human sin in this world, faith believes
that His purpose shall be perfectly fulfilled hereafter;
and hope looks in quiet confidence to that fulfilment
and thus 'in quietness and in confidence shall be our
strength.' [1]

[1] Isa. xxx. 15.

CHAPTER VI

THE NEW MAN AND THE OLD

'*Ye have not so learned Christ; if so be that ye have heard Him, and have been taught by Him, as the truth is in Jesus: that ye put off concerning the former conversa .on the old man, which is corrupt according to the deceitful lusts; and be renewed in the spirit of your mind; and that ye put on the new man, which after God is created in righteousness and true holiness.*'—EPH. iv. 20-24.

THESE strong and carefully phrased words of S. Paul are quite familiar to us, but, since they occur in the context of serious and gross sin, perhaps we do not always take them to our hearts as we should; yet they are fundamental to the whole of our spiritual life.

We have been trying to understand something of 'the new man which after God is created in righteousness and true holiness,' new with all that newness which lifts us above the natural man and makes us so much more than anything we could possibly be by ourselves, which is not dependent upon our own effort nor won by our own goodness, but which is given by the love and mercy of God; that given newness which is ours in Christ.

Because we have within us this new man, we are capable of something of which we were not capable before—perfection. 'Be ye therefore perfect,' says

our Lord, and His words are a command to us all;
but the perfection He would see in us is not any
sort of human perfection—for Christian spirituality
is not a spiritual gymnastic for the production of
supermen—but a divine perfection. 'Be ye perfect,'
He says, not humanly but 'as your Father in heaven
is perfect,'[1] with the perfection of the sons of God.
The whole possibility of such perfection flows from
the new nature which is given to us in the Catholic
Church; it may be ours, not because we are in
ourselves wonderful people or spiritual athletes, for
we know only too well that we are neither, but
because God our Father has given to us of His own
fullness[2] and we are 'created after God in righteousness and true holiness.' God calls us to perfection
because we are His sons.

Now it is one thing to be a son and quite another
to be a good son; it is one thing to be a branch of
the Vine and another to be a fruitful branch; one
thing to be united to Christ and quite another to
be like Him. How easy it is to test the truth of this
statement. We do not have to look far before we
find people who could be so much better, who should
be reflecting something of the perfection of God,
but who are yet quite content to be careless, mediocre
Christians; people who should be so big content to
be so small. We see some who pride themselves
on being very correct Catholics but are at the same
time quite empty of that which should above all
characterize the Catholic, charity; others who keep
themselves scrupulously from the grosser and more
obvious sins but are nevertheless full of pride, envy,

[1] S. Matt. v. 48.   [2] S. John i. 16.

E

jealousy, and all the spiritual sins which negate the
whole character of God. It is one thing to be a
son, but quite another to be a good son.

Our Lord is the perfect Son of God, and if we
would be likewise perfect we must learn Christ as
S. Paul assumes the Ephesians have done. S. Paul's
words are remarkable, for he says to them, 'That ye
have heard Him and been taught by Him as the
truth is in Jesus.' The Apostle was not writing to
the first generation of Jews who had seen and
heard Jesus in the flesh, he was writing to dwellers
in the Greek and heathen city of Ephesus to which
our Lord had never been, and yet he says, 'Ye have
heard Him and been taught by Him.' Evidently
this hearing and teaching must be something which
we in our generation can share with the Ephesians
of his, and the reference is not to the earthly life
of our Lord at all. It is to the instruction of the
glorified Christ that we must give ear, Christ teaching us through His Body the Church and through
the inspiration of the Spirit, teaching us not only
about Himself but teaching us *Himself* Who is the
Truth. 'Truth is found in the Person of Jesus, Who
is the Christ: He is Himself the Truth (*S. John* xiv.
6): hence we can be said to "learn Him." '[1] And
in Him we learn the secret of good sonship.

But the Pauline teaching does not stop there, the
effect of learning Christ is to induce us to put on the
new man; it must not be merely or even primarily
theoretical, but must have the practical end of
making us good sons of God. The new man is given

[1] J. Armitage Robinson, *S. Paul's Epistle to the Ephesians*,
ad loc.

to us by God, it is our new being, but it must nevertheless be put on, and that putting on is our own act. We cannot get on with a passive acceptance of the divine gift. That gift to become effective demands a radical response of our whole being, a deliberate putting on of newness, a purposeful identification of ourselves with the divine Son; for S. Paul does not only tell us to put on the new man, he also tells us to put on Christ[1] Who Himself is the new Man, the root and principle of all our newness. We have been brought into the fellowship of the Holy Catholic Church, we have heard and been taught and learned (or have begun to learn), and it is ours to put on the new man which is Christ if we would walk worthily of the vocation wherewith we are called.

The likeness to God which is given to us must be developed by our own act, it is our part to respond to the Holy Spirit in that development freely and generously. God must be all if His gifts are to come to perfection in us. That demands the complete response of the whole man with no half measures about it. There are far too many people about who seek to temporize, who try to make the best of both worlds of grace and of nature without giving themselves wholly to either, nevertheless it cannot be done. We cannot go on sitting on the fence indefinitely; either the old man will assert himself or the new man will be put on, it must be one or the other; and the answer as to which it is to be rests with us.

Our part in our perfection is a freely and deliber-

[1] Rom. xiii. 14.

ately willed response to the movement of God. God has given us new being and new life, He fills us with His Spirit; we must identify ourselves wholly with all that, we must respond, otherwise we receive the gift of God indeed, but receive it in vain.

God does not work in us by cancelling out our personalities but by perfecting them and making them conformable to His perfect will, yet He does not do this by taking an automatic control over us, so that all we have to do is to slide through life without any further trouble; the putting on of the new man demands the surrender, in generous response to God, of all that we have and are.

The work of our salvation is the result of interaction between the will of God and the will of man. It is the will of God that matters, for He is our prime Mover and final End and we can do nothing apart from Him; it is our part to identify ourselves as fully as possible with His will, giving ourselves to that purpose that we may fulfil the end for which God has made us. Without that there can be no perfection.

Our perfection, then, depends upon a real, willed, loving devotion to the will of God, and it is just that which is often so sadly to seek in us. What we want does not matter at all, what He wants matters infinitely, but we seldom realize this.

Our trouble lies frequently in the fact that we identify the will of God exclusively with what is unpleasant. Popular hymnology has done much to cloud the issue in this matter. 'Thy way not mine, O Lord,' and other compositions of a similar kind have produced a morbid view of the matter comparable to that of the lady who, on being told by the Captain during a storm at sea that they must just put themselves in the hand of God, replied, 'Good gracious, surely it can't be as bad as that!' It is true that the hymn I have noticed does mention the other side of the matter and is perhaps intended to be a balanced statement of our position; but it is the dark side of the picture which stands out in the popular mind to the almost complete exclusion of the light, which is after all the more important and fundamental. The will of God is our supreme good, not our supreme misery; in His will is our peace, not our torment; but it only becomes our peace when we identify ourselves with it, so long as we resist or disobey it it is truly our torment, which is then our own fault. When we attain to a real devotion to the divine will and a true love of it, when we desire it above all things because we love God our Father above all, then are we beginning to become good sons.

But it is precisely here that our difficulty lies. Grace completes and reorientates nature, but it does not destroy it, and the nature which it completes is not nature as God created it but nature as man has spoiled it, the fallen, warped human nature that we know so well—the old man.

The old man is reunited with God, but he is still there to be reckoned with and he will remain there until the last breath we draw in this world. Some people look forward to a time when they will arrive at a comfortable state of holiness in which they will not have to do any more fighting; it is a natural hope but a vain one, for the old man is there and will

continue to make a nuisance of himself, there will
always be need of that austere thing which the
theologians call mortification. It is a hard thing
but, whether we like it or not, it is a necessary thing,
and no one can be a good Christian without it. We
cannot be anything in this world which is worth
while without mortification of some sort, still less
can we be that most wonderful thing of all, a man
or woman approaching perfection. There is the old
man and he must be put off, as S. Paul says; there
must be no identification of the will with him.
That means hard, steady self-denial.

The life which we live with Christ in this world is
a new life, a risen life. S. Paul in another place
says that we are risen with Christ, and goes on to
draw this conclusion: 'If ye then be risen with
Christ, seek those things which are above, where
Christ sitteth on the right hand of God. Set your
affection on things above, not on things on the earth.
For ye are dead, and your life is hid with Christ in
God. . . . Mortify therefore your members which
are upon the earth.'[1]

That is what is symbolized in the ceremonial of
Holy Baptism; the neophyte goes down into the
water and is submerged, buried, he ascends out of
the water a new man to a new life; the old man is
put to death that the new man may be raised up.
He is risen with Christ now, he does not look to a
future resurrection of this kind, and his life is hid
with Christ in God.

But that which is symbolized in Baptism as a
single act has to be actualized in daily life. The

[1] Col. iii. 1-3, 5.

putting to death of the old man and the raising up of the new are continually going on in our experience, and if we are to attain to perfection it will be upon the corpse of that old man who is somehow or other always contriving to be alive.

What, then, are the marks of the old man? First of all pride, that pride which makes self the end of action instead of God, which is thinking always of what I want, whether this thing or person appeals to or displeases me. And, arising out of that pride, self-will; the seeking of oneself, one's own desires, one's advancement, comfort, or pleasure, whether in temporal things or spiritual. All this is the setting of self in the place which should be for God alone, for He Who made us should be the end of our actions; all else is self-idolatry, and if that be our mind we can hardly be surprised that our desires get out of order.

Man as God created him was, whatever else he may have been, at least one whose desires were in the right order, God first and all else in God. By sin we have destroyed that order and, placing self first, have put a whole medley of things between us and the divine will. We can hardly be surprised that those errant desires of ours are so troublesome or that our souls become chaotic and we wander about not knowing whither we are bound.

But along with that goes an even worse thing, the real love of sin. There is not one of us but has some sin which he loves. We may pretend otherwise or excuse ourselves by saying that it is only a very little one; perhaps it is not so little as we like to think.

Some philosophers who try to grapple with the

problem of evil feel the difficulty of accounting for
it so acutely that they try to explain it as exclusively
a negative thing with no positive existence at all.
That may be all very well in the construction of a
nice square philosophical theory but it is not a full
account of reality. We all know evil as a positive
fact and our liking for it as equally positive; it is
there, part of the old man, and we have to learn by
the grace of God to eradicate it. There is the old
man putting self first, and in consequence of that
initial evil falling into confusion of desire and the
love of the wrong thing, and he, as S. Paul shows
us, must be crucified and kept on his cross.

It is only by mortification that we can put on the
new man and crucify the old, and its purpose is not
merely the crucifixion of the one but even more the
raising up of the other, for the new man can only
rise on the death of the old. The two things go
together and together form part of a continuous
process.

Our pride has got to be overcome, but that can
only be by learning humility, that true and sweet
humility which is not just a piece of pietistic insin-
cerity but actually the seeing of ourselves as we are
and acting accordingly. This all depends upon our
vision of God. If we have begun to see God as He
is, to know Him, and realize that He is all and that
we are nothing apart from Him and His love, then we
must see that our self-sufficiency and self-will are
just things which have to be thrown away because
we are not the great people we sometimes like to
think we are but the little children of God.

Humility must lead on to the emptying of self-will out of our hearts. We want, or we should want, to be filled with God; but we cannot be filled with God if we are already half or three-quarters full of self, we can only be filled with Him if we are empty. So there must be an emptying of self, not in order to create a vacuum or to provide pleasant lodgings for seven more devils, but to make room in our hearts, our minds, our wills, for the All-holy God.

That is what the saints mean by the noughting of self; not the abrogation of our personality (which so many people think they mean) but the excision of pride, self-will, and the love of sin, the crucifixion of the old man.

That means daily mortification, daily discipline of self. 'If any man will come after Me,' says our Lord, 'let him deny himself, and take up his cross daily, and follow Me.'[1] He is not speaking of saints, He says 'any man'; He is not speaking of a single act, He says 'daily.' That constant taking up of the cross, that discipline, that mortification is the very mark of the Christian, the follower of Jesus, the member of Christ and Son of God.

But notice that our Lord says 'take up his cross.' That is what we will not do; we rebel against discipline, we fight against it, or we turn from the cross which God places upon our shoulders to a self-chosen one which is more attractive and less heavy, and so we miss the God-given means of our sanctification and the privilege of bearing the Cross of Christ after Him. The fact is that in this cross-bearing we are each one of us Simon of Cyrene.

[1] S. Luke ix. 23.

The Cross which we bear is not ours but Christ's,
and He Himself bears the other end.

If now instead of rebelling against the Cross we
accept it, take it up, if not with joy like the saints,
at least with some cheerfulness, we shall find that
God in His own way is disciplining our souls as He
alone can, is aiding us in that difficult business of the
supersession of the old man and making our soul
the sort of being in which His virtues can blossom.

Discipline, mortification, finds its issue in loving,
generous, cheerful obedience to the divine will.
'If ye love Me, keep My commandments';[1] there is
no other way, no other mark of love than that.
No pleasantness in prayer, no height in devotion
can show forth our love to God without the humble,
costing actions of obedience, and it is as we give
ourselves in obedience to the will of God in the
details of everyday life, as we learn to hold our wills
in His and care less about our own, so we may be
given whole and entire to God and it may become
more possible for us to say with the Apostle, 'I live;
yet not I, but Christ liveth in me.'[2]   So will the old
man be put off and the new man put on.

[1] S. John xiv. 15.   [2] Gal. ii. 20.

CHAPTER VII

PRAYER

'Pray without ceasing.'—I THESS. v. 17.

SPIRITUAL writers tell us that there are two
wings whereby the soul ascends to God; the one
is mortification, which we have already considered,
and the other prayer, with which we are about to
deal. Many people fail to see the connection between these two wings, with the result that many
who delight in prayer, at least when it is full of
fervour and joy, either ignore mortification altogether or regard themselves as superior to it, with
disastrous results. It is impossible to fly with one
wing; if we would truly rise to God we must use
both.

'Both these duties of mortification and prayer are so
absolutely necessary that they must neither of them ever
cease, but continually increase in perfection and virtue
to the end of our lives. For though self-love and pride
may by mortification be subdued, yet as long as we are
imprisoned in mortal bodies of flesh and blood, they will
never be totally rooted out of us, but that even the most
perfect souls will find in themselves matter enough for
further mortification. And again, our union with God
by prayer can never either be so constant but that it will
be interrupted, so as that the soul will fall from her
height back some degrees into nature again; nor is there
any degree of it so perfect, pure, and spiritual, but that

it may, and by exercise will, become yet more and more
pure without limits.

The diligent exercise of each of these doth much
advance the practice of the other.   For as mortification
is a good disposition to prayer, yea, so necessary that a
sensual immortified soul cannot raise herself up so much
as to look to God with any cordial desire to please Him,
or to love and be resigned to Him, much less to be
perfectly united to Him; so, likewise, by prayer the
soul obtains light to discover whatsoever inordinate
affections in her are to be mortified, and also strength
of spiritual grace actually and effectually to subdue
them. . . . Mortification without prayer will be but
superficial, or, it is to be feared, hypocritical; and
prayer, with a neglect of mortification, will be heartless,
distracted, and of small virtue.' [1]

So we see how necessary the one wing is to the
other.

Prayer is a common human activity.   Prayer of
some kind is to be found wherever men are, but it
differs vastly in degree; there is all the difference
in the world between the Tibetan prayer-wheel and
the contemplation of the Christian saint.   The root
of these differences lies in the character of the
religion of the person praying and of his belief in
God.   The higher the religion and the nearer its
approach to the worship of the true God, the higher
in general will be its prayer; so the prayers of the
West African animist, the Hindu, the Buddhist, the
Mohammedan may be said to form a sort of ascend-
ing series.   But when we come to Christian prayer
we find that, while it has affinities with the prayer
of other religions, as it must have since it is part

[1] Augustine Baker, *Holy Wisdom*, Tr. II, sect. 1,
chap. i. 6, 7, 9.

of human prayer, yet it differs from them not only
in degree but in kind. This is so, not because
Christians are superior to other men as men but
because as members of Christ and children of God
we have been brought by the grace and mercy and
love of God into such a relationship with Him that
our prayer changes in character; it is no longer
merely creaturely, though it still remains that, but
it is the prayer of sons. There is, then, a peculiar
quality in Christian prayer which differentiates it
from other prayer, and that is because it is the out-
come of that which gives us new life and new being,
the grace of God.

Now S. Paul gives us a very categorical admonition
in regard to prayer, which consists of only three
words (two in Greek) and has no qualification whatsoever, 'Pray without ceasing.' If we take that to
our hearts as we should do, the first thing which
strikes us is the extreme difficulty of fulfilling it.
One's first reaction is to say, 'Well, of course that
may be all very well for monks and nuns who have
nothing else to do, but it is quite impossible for me,
living in the world as I do, to pray without ceasing;
and when I do come to prayer, though I give what
time to it I can, I do so little, and what I do is so
bad.'

That sort of reaction is quite natural. But it is
mistaken. S. Paul was not writing to monks and
nuns, for the very good reason that there were none
for him to write to, he was writing to perfectly
ordinary Christians living in a busy city and to very
young Christians at that. The First Epistle to the
Thessalonians was probably written about A.D. 51,

when those to whom it was addressed had only been
converted a few months. They were not therefore
saints to whom the Apostle wrote this startling thing
but beginners, and what he said to them was not
that they should give as much time as they could
spare to prayer but that they should pray without
ceasing, which is quite a different thing.

If we want a higher authority than S. Paul we may
remind ourselves that his Master once spoke an
arresting parable about an unjust judge and a poor
woman who would not leave him alone, and S. Luke
tells us that His purpose was to show us 'that men
ought always to pray and not to faint.'[1]

Now our Lord and S. Paul after Him show us by
these sayings that prayer is not just one of the things
which we do because it is in our rule of life. We
make a rule of life and we tick the things off one by
one—work, rest, recreation, food, almsgiving, mortification, etc., public worship, and prayer. But
prayer is not just one point among many: it is the
one thing which is vital to all Christian living, the
very breath of the soul.

You may make your Communion, and there is
no sort of doubt that you have truly received our
Lord with all the blessings that He brings with Him,
and yet your reception of the Blessed Sacrament
may be quite sterile because you yourself have failed
in prayer. You may do something for God, really
for Him, and it may look on the outside as though
it were a success, but it is spiritually a failure, it does
not effect God's real purpose because it has not been
animated by prayer. You may be living a perfectly

[1] S. Luke xviii. 1.

correct Catholic life exteriorly, and yet be far away from God because you are neglecting prayer. That is what is happening over and over again all over the country. We find parishes which ought to be successes and are actually failures, not because there is a lack of goodwill or activity but because there is a lack of prayer; the leaves are there, a full church, plenty of organizations, endless meetings, but somehow or other the fruit does not mature, because the people, and still more the priests, do not pray continually.

You can always tell the churches in which people pray; they may not be so showy, they do not go in for 'stunts,' they may even be lacking in organizations; but they are alive, throbbing with that quality of silence which comes from continual commerce with the Most High, spiritual power-houses through which the Holy Ghost accomplishes His purpose in a sinful world. Prayer truly is the most important thing in life.

Then we must pray; but how can we pray better? That is a question which can be answered ultimately for the individual alone; each one of us is different, and only the soul, its spiritual director, and the Holy Spirit know in detail what is best for each. What can be done here is to lay down certain principles which may act as guides to prayer.

If we are to arrive at good prayer we must first of all consider what is likely to be the cause of our present imperfection, and the first cause of our feebleness, indeed the persistent cause, is the weakness of our wills. It is so easy to make up our minds that we are going to do so much praying and when it comes to the point it is equally easy to find some apparently good reason why we should not do it. There is a particular sort of barrage which the devil puts up when we would come to prayer, which we all know but which we get caught in time after time, the barrage of disinclination, the hardness and unattractiveness of the whole thing, the emptiness of our soul, or the importance of something else which we think ought to be done at that moment. There is no need to fuss over that sort of difficulty, it must just be disregarded and worked through; if we allow our wills to get feeble over it we shall not pray and the only gainer will be the devil. Our wills are so weak and our love of God so slender that we get caught in that old trap time after time; what is needed is steady perseverance.

There may also be a failure to realize what we are really about when we pray. It is, I believe, true that we commonly teach our children to say prayers rather than to pray, with the result that they grow up with the idea that the important thing is to say certain words morning and night, and consequently, if they do not give up, they go on 'saying their prayers' to the end of their lives. This leads to two dangers, the first of formalism, the notion that so long as one says certain forms of words, often with little reference to the applicability of the forms, one has prayed; so we get the grown man still praying to be made a good boy and even worse misfits. Such prayer tends to become a little magic which we would not do without but which has little intelligible meaning or relation to life. The other danger is that of thinking that prayer consists wholly of speech, whereas it may not. Prayer is far more than the words we use in it; words are not of the essence of prayer though they may be a very necessary and important part of it.

The ...re is also a contrary danger to be visualized ... Many people who are advancing a little in ... or think they are doing so, imagine that they ... ense with saying anything at all; that is not ... ever get to a point when we can safely do ... th words altogether. When our way of ... hanges we naturally use words in a different ... may use fewer words, but we must go on ... m in the way which is right for us. It is ... sible to pray very well indeed without saying ... for a long time, there is no need to be ... lly talking like a gossiping woman when one ... to the presence of God, and the more one ... reverences Him the less likely one is to ... do that. Economy of words is the natural ... of a lover; when two lovers are together ... often spend long periods when they will say ... at all and yet be completely satisfied, and ... not, as some cynics think, because they are ... but because the converse of their mutual ... e is something deeper and more satisfying ... much speech; nevertheless speech has its place, ... will not always be silent. So it is with the soul ... loves God, it will know when to speak and when ... be silent and its silence will often mean more than ... eech; if that be so it is clear that prayer is vastly ... ore than saying prayers.

If prayer is more than words so also is it more than ...ere asking. Of course there is and must always

be much petition in prayer, the very realization o
God's perfection and our need is in itself a petition
but prayer is more than that and petition must itsel
depend upon something else, otherwise it may b
simply selfish, just going to God for what
get as small nephews seek to extract tips
benevolent uncle. But we cannot treat G
that, petition must never have the firs
behind it, however great our need, mus
'nevertheless' of Jesus, that perfect devotion
of God, 'nevertheless not as I will but as Th

Another reason for our feebleness in p
in the undue multiplication of aids to it.
finds many people who, when they come
prayers, bring with them armies of littl
when they come to their intercessions prod
long lists; when they come to their medit
themselves up in elaborate methods, and
behave like the White Knight who enc
himself with much variegated luggage the on
of which was to keep him constantly falling
horse he was supposed to be riding. Of co
these things are necessary to a certain ext
for certain people, but they are not pray
multiplied beyond necessity they only get in t
and make that which should be simple mo
necessarily complicated.

A similar danger which attacks some people is
of getting so interested in their own soul's process
that they never get beyond them; so that instea
of contemplating God and finding Him they merel
contemplate themselves.

[1] S. Matt. xxvi. 39.

If we are really to pray we must refuse to allow ourselves to become immersed in the secondary and we must only use it as the best means at our disposal of arriving at the root of the matter.

What, then, is prayer? The lifting up of the soul to God. A child can remember that, and happy is the child who has been taught it. 'Yes,' you may say, 'I know that but it does not seem to get me any further.' I think, however, that if you consider it carefully you will find that this easy definition gets you very far indeed.

In the first place, prayer is a lifting up; that means that whatever else it may be and whatever its form may be prayer is essentially an act of the will. As the soul becomes more unified its prayer becomes more simply willed, which accounts for the apparent bareness of contemplation; but in all prayer it is the will which matters.

There are in this action two necessary parts: recollection and concentration. Recollection in this sense is the gathering together of one's whole self, detaching one's desires and interests from all other things and placing oneself whole and entire at the feet of God. It is the failure to do this which produces much distracted and superficial praying. We may be on our knees, we may be saying words, but our real selves may be far away; it is only as we gather our whole selves up to one point that we can be said really to pray. Being recollected, we then seek to concentrate all our attention upon God.

This brings us to the second point of our definition, which is that God is the end of every prayer we pray. Every moment of our prayer time must be

soul which never wholly pours itself out on things created but lives increasingly in God.

The prayerful, recollected man is not one who is always thinking about God—that is impossible in this world—but one who never intentionally withdraws from Him, whose prayer supplies a supernatural motive for the whole of life and every action in life, of whatever kind that action may be. So through the growing perfection of our acts of prayer we enter into a state of soul in which, consciously or unconsciously, God Himself is the end of our living, and we thus truly pray continually.

CHAPTER VIII

WORSHIP

'The Lord shall ye fear and Him shall ye worship.'
2 KINGS xvii. 36.

WORSHIP is so fundamentally characteristic of
religion that there can be no true religion
without it, and that because it is the inevitable
response of the creature to his God. The moment
we realize God as God we are irresistibly impelled
to offer Him our worship; so the three disciples in
face of the wonderful revelation of the Transfiguration fell on their faces, as did S. Paul when he
beheld the vision on the Damascus road.

This is a fact which is not only forgotten but
frequently denied. Religion in the popular mind
is identified with edification and personal well-being.
So a man goes to church for his own satisfaction, and
if he is not satisfied he stays away because, as he
says, he can worship God in the open air as well as
in church; a statement which, while it does indeed
recognize that worship is of the essence of the matter,
yet cuts at its root, for he does not go into the open
air (or golf course) to worship God but to please
himself.

It is perhaps not unduly pessimistic to remark that
among regular church-goers there is but a small

percentage who really put the worship of God in the
first place. Music, ceremonial, preaching are all
ancillary to worship, but there is a constant danger
of putting them and the personal delight which can
be gained from them first and the worship of God
second.

Worship is the essentially godward action of the
human soul; it is the one thing which we do simply
and solely for God with no other end in view at all;
it is the action of adoration whereby we glorify God
for His own sake, the gathering up of the whole self
in faith, hope, and love, and the offering of that self
to His glory.

All creation glorifies God by fulfilling His purpose.
Earth, stars, plants, animals, magnify Him by being
what they are, and all the ecstasy of the *Benedicite*
is witness to that fact; but man, because he is a
reasonable being, glorifies Him by the deliberate act
of worship. It is because we are men that we are
able, that we are required, to worship the Most
High.

In previous chapters we have considered what we
are as Christians, but if we are to gain a true understanding of worship we must go a step further and
inquire what we are as men.

There are many levels of being in the world, each
with its own distinctive quality. Thus the plant is
distinguished from the mineral by its inherent life
which is, as it were, a new irruption into creation
lifting it on to a new sphere of being; the animal, is
distinguished from the plant by its sentience, another
new beginning and a still higher level of being; with
man creation attains to a higher level yet, and

another new beginning, that of spirit, for that which differentiates man from the rest of the world is the fact that he is a spiritual being.

The true characteristic of man is not that part of him which is akin to the animal creation but that which he shares with the angels, his spirit; and worship is the response of the created spirit to the Spirit of God, an essentially spiritual act.

This is why so many fail in it. It is easy enough to live on a sub-spiritual level and many people do it quite happily; but to live spiritually needs discipline and training. Until God has been perceived spiritually it is impossible to begin to realize Him as He truly is, and the nature and necessity of worship is misunderstood. But once He has been so perceived there is no question about it; the soul sees and adores, it is the natural result of the meeting of the human spirit with its God.

The worshipping man is he who enters into the spiritual heritage of his being, and this, as we have seen, needs discipline and training if it is to be characteristic of the whole man as it should be. But that does not mean that worship is confined to saints; God reveals Himself to large numbers who are not yet saints, indeed there are probably very few Christian souls who are in earnest about their religion to whom He has not revealed Himself; the trouble is that they do not always respond to that revelation by persevering love. It is difficult truly to seek God and nothing less.

Worship, then, is a spiritual act, the response to God which we share with the angels; but we are not angels, and so long as we inhabit this planet our worship is not wholly spiritual. Many good people have thought that it is, or should ideally be so, and have consequently sought to strip worship of all that appeals to the senses and to make it a solely interior thing; but in seeking such an ideal they have desired an impossibility which is contrary to the nature which the Lord God has given us.

God has given us for so long as we dwell in this world a nature which is not pure spirit, nor even incarnate spirit, but one which is made up of two dissimilar elements, body and soul. It is convenient, indeed necessary, to distinguish one from the other in thought, but though we can legitimately so isolate them theoretically, in practice they are inseparable. No willed action, not even the most instinctive, is purely physical or purely spiritual; we can never say exactly where spirit ends and body begins, because the two together form one organism. Without the soul the body is dead; without the body the soul cannot express itself; and whether we like it or whether we do not God has created body and soul as a unity which is only separable at death.

It is true that striving saints have felt most deeply and said most emphatically that the body is the prison-house of the soul, but that is hardly an adequate account of their relationship. When S. Augustine says that man is 'a mind using a body' that is Platonism not Christianity, and in that matter the Christian must part company with Plato. Because he saw this so clearly S. Thomas Aquinas followed Aristotle rather than Plato in his philosophy of the being of man, in spite of the fact that

the Aristotelian theory by itself produced grave
difficulties of another kind.

Man is a unity of body and soul, a sacrament
whose outward sign can never in this world be
separated from the inward part. We can, if we
know him well enough, forecast from a person's
character the sort of thing which he will do or not
do under certain circumstances, because his outward
actions are the expression of his spiritual being, his
real self. There are, then, in man two kinds of
being which interact on account of their organic
unity, the spiritual and the material, and these two
together make up man as he is.

If this is a true account of our being it follows that
the idea of worship as purely spiritual and interior
is mistaken because, in this life, man is body and
spirit and no action of his belongs wholly and simply
to one side of his nature. Worship is an act of which
only spiritual beings are capable but, in the case of
man, it is not purely spiritual because man is not
pure spirit, so that, even if he were capable of purely
spiritual activity, such activity would be the work
of but part of himself, the most important part
certainly but only part when all is said and done.

Worship must be the act of the whole man, its
bodily expression is not accidental but necessary,
not only as the expression of the spirit's act but as the
homage of the body joined to that of the spirit.

Further, if the spirit uses the body as its means
of expression it also gains from the body increase
of devotion; recollectedness, for instance, is greatly
assisted and partly created by bodily posture, the
actual saying of prayers and singing of psalms and

hymns increase fervour. So, as S. Thomas says, 'The human mind stands in need of the guidance of the sensible in that whereby it is conjoined to God (that is, the exercises of religion); for "the invisible things of Him are clearly seen, being understood by the things that are made" (*Rom*. i. 20). Therefore the use of corporal things is necessary to the worship of God as a sign whereby the mind of man may be excited to spiritual acts whereby it is conjoined to God. Religion, then, requires principally certain interior acts which belong to it *per se*, and secondarily exterior acts ordinated to them.'[1]

True worship, then, must be exterior as well as interior, bodily as well as spiritual, that it may be the most complete homage of the whole self, and the worship of the Church provides for this. The liturgy is not merely the saying of certain prayers and the reading of certain passages of Scripture, but an action which consists in the saying and doing of certain prescribed things at certain times for a certain end. These words and actions are necessary to the act of worship, not accretions which have become attached to it, and the action is the offering of the worship of the whole man, spirit and body, to his God.

If words and actions are thus necessary to worship so also is the House of God, and that not only because if a number of people are to be gathered together there must be somewhere to gather them, some common meeting-place, but because of man's religious needs as man. Man has always been a temple-builder and God Himself has deigned to call

[1] *Summa Theologica*, IIa, IIae, Q. lxxxi, art. 7.

a man-made building His House; obviously this is
not necessary on God's side, for the Infinite is
independent of all space, but on our side it is necessary. A place wherein we can find God is essential
to us if we are to find Him everywhere, we need a
meeting-place between ourselves and the Most High
hallowed by association with the holiest moments
of God's people and their realization of His presence,
a place set apart for His worship, the House of His
presence. God does not dwell in temples made with
hands as though He needed them, but because we
need them.

So too because of our need the Lord Who in-
habiteth eternity deigns to come to His temple and
dwell in it for us, and Jesus gives us His Presence in
the Blessed Sacrament. It is easy to think of His
sacramental Presence as being 'localized' in a false
way as though He were confined within the elements,
so that when they are absent He Himself is not there,
and exaggerated language of this kind has done
untold harm. We can, however, say truly that we
finite, human beings are by reason of our nature
incapable of adequate worship of a God Who is
everywhere in general and nowhere in particular;
we need not only some place where we can find and
worship Him but some mode of His presence which
is, as it were, fitted to our need in that place; so our
Lord gives us His presence not only for our food but
also for our worship in material and spatial species.
He Who is everywhere 'comes' in special to this
place that we may find and adore Him there.

We have been considering worship primarily as a
human action, the homage of man to God, but to

the Christian this homage is deepened into sacrifice, the sacrifice of the whole man. Christian worship, therefore, is consummated not simply in the worship of our Lord in the Blessed Sacrament but in the offering of Him in the Mass. That sacrifice which our Lord Himself is always pleading in heaven He gives to the Church to plead on earth and in that pleading we all have our part; in it Christ, His Body, and His members are all one, and by entering into that sacrifice and joining ourselves with it we make to God that perfect act of worship, of homage, by which we are wholly given to Him.

This leads us to the truth that Christian worship is never a purely individual thing. The Christian is what he is because he is a member of the Body of Christ, not because he is himself outstandingly spiritual or holy. He does not approach God as an isolated unit, or as one unit in the company of others, but as part of the Church. Part but not a mere part, for he does not surrender his personality in thus worshipping, rather he expands it. Taken singly we are insignificant (though precious as persons in the sight of God), and our worship suffers from the effects of our sins and imperfections, but as members of Christ we take our place in the worship of His Body, the place which is reserved for ourselves and no others in the will of God. We bring to that offering all the devotion of which we are capable, our poor little bit of love, and put it into the great common stock of the Church, and our worship is thus raised above itself and united with that of the whole Body of Christ on earth, in purgatory and in heaven, and with Christ Himself, to find itself

transfigured in that great homage; the worship of
the whole man in the whole Christ.

There are many devout souls whose spiritual life
is wrapped up in their own private prayers; they go
to Mass indeed, but as individuals, they are hardly
conscious of the real corporateness of the action in
which they are taking part, and leave most of the
actual action to others. Their corporate devotion,
such as it is, is built upon their personal. The last
thing we would wish to do is to decry personal
devotion and worship, rather would we see it increase
and deepen, for the devotion of the Church depends
upon the devotion of its members and there is no
such thing as corporate devotion in the abstract apart
from them; but, as we have said, no Christian is a
mere unit, his devotion depends upon his union
with Christ in His Body; it must, then, be broad-
based upon the worship of that Body.

The great Benedictine tradition, enshrining as it
does the spiritual wisdom of the early Church and
the ages of faith, bears constant witness to this truth.
For S. Benedict and his sons it is the *Opus Dei*, the
Mass and Office, which is the heart of all devotion,
the great action to which all else must be subordinate
and from which all else proceeds; to that all personal
devotion is brought, from that all personal devotion
is nourished. That principle is not peculiar to
monks, though they by reason of their vocation and
manner of life practise it in its fullness as those in
the world cannot do, but it should be common to
all the members of Christ's Body.

The worship of the Church does not always make
a personal appeal, indeed its characteristic is to be

upra-personal, and for that reason the individual
may find it tiresome or jejune; that, however, is no
eason for avoiding it, rather does it provide a
personal offering of great value. We do not worship
God to please ourselves but to adore Him, and
adoration is a costing thing. But our dissatisfaction
arises most frequently from a misunderstanding of
he action in which we are taking part. The litur-
gical worship of the Church of S. Sophronius, Mud-
horpe, may be very inadequately offered, it may be
dull and unedifying, but we must not allow our minds
to be bounded by the four walls of S. Sophronius.
t is not with just that handful of uninteresting people
hat we are worshipping God but with the whole
Church living, departed, and glorified, and the angels
and archangels are as truly present there as in the
most glorious house of God in which His worship is
offered most perfectly. It is not just this dull
Evensong at which we are assisting but the worship
of the whole Catholic Church. The worship of the
Church began on the day on which she was born and
t has never ceased, there is never a moment, day
nor night, in which Mass is not being said in some
part of the world; as the sun pursues his westering
round he calls priest after priest to the altar to offer
he Holy Sacrifice, and the worship of the Divine
Office is never stilled. It is into that action that we
enter when we join in the Church's worship, not
to be lost in it but to take our part, to make it. That
thought should inspire us to devotion when outward
conditions militate against it.

Membership of the Body of Christ does not only
give us a place in the worship of that Body, it also

gives a new character to our private and personal
worship, for we do not divest ourselves of that
membership when we worship God in the privacy
of our own room or the stillness of some church.   It
is not as single human beings that we worship Him
at all, but as living parts of His Church, and that
Church is lifted up to Him by our adoration and
adores Him in us.   We cannot, then, think of 'our
prayers' as though they were something individual
and private, or of ourselves as 'alone with the Alone.'
We are indeed alone with God in a true sense, but
in us the Church is alone with Him and we are, as it
were, adoring points of contact between Him and
her.   Every act of adoration has thus an intercessory
value even though it may not be a specific act of
intercession;   the prayer, the adoration of the
individual, has its effect upon the whole Body.

Adoration not only unites the individual soul with
God but also with the whole Church.   Clearly, then,
we must give ourselves to adoring prayer not only
on our own account but on hers.   The contempla-
tive orders of religious derive their *raison d'être* from
this fact.   Contemplatives are very far from being the
selfish people they are constantly accused of being,
rather are they those who hold the whole Church
within the will of God by their ceaseless adoration
of Him, who by their prayer bring the grace of God
to those who do not pray; and we in the world who
seek to draw as close to God as we may in prayer
are, in our degree, doing identically the same
thing.

But we must go a step further.   If worship is the
adoration of the whole man united to Christ and His

Church it is also the service of his whole life and not merely part of it.

We constantly draw a hard-and-fast line between prayer and life, sacred and secular; a line which God has not drawn and which robs life of its true significance. Worship, strictly so-called, is, as we have seen, an exclusively godward act in which we seek no other end but His glory and adore Him with our whole selves; it is upon that action that our whole life should be founded, an action which, if it is real, must influence all else. But worship does not end there, it must pass from adoration to service, from deliberate action to a constant state of will. It is the same individual that prays, worships, works, and plays; the same life that he lives whatever he may be doing at any particular moment of it. We cannot divide our being and life into sections. The act of adoration is the orientation not only of that particular moment but of the whole life towards God: we may not regard the time of worship as something snatched for more serious employ out of a life predominantly engaged otherwise, nor as a token-payment of our duty towards God, for worship and the rest of life do not stand over against one another as separate and dissimilar entities. Worship is the hallowing of life that all may become worshipful. So we pass from the act of worship to that of service whereby all life is directed to the glory of God and every action tends to that end; thus is the will of God fulfilled in this world not only in actions specifically religious but in all things.

The archangel in introducing himself to Tobit said, 'I am Raphael, one of the seven holy angels, which present the prayers of the saints, and which go in and out before the glory of the Holy One.'[1] We share with the angels the same vocation, to go in before the glory of the Holy One in worship, to go out with that same glory as our objective; so does our life attain not merely a material but a spiritual end, and so are our actions, even the most mundane and apparently unreligious ones, spiritualized and the transitory life of earth linked with the eternal life of heaven. If thus we work and play and eat and sleep for God, life, however drab, humble, or miserable in itself, becomes transfigured with the glory of God Who gave it.

[1] Tobit xii. 15.

CHAPTER IX

THE LOVE OF GOD

'*My beloved is mine, and I am His.*'—Song of Songs ii. 16.

THE foundation of the Christian life is, as we have seen, God's gift of Himself to us and the planting within us of a supernatural capacity for that gift. But the gift can never be wholly appropriated in this life, however great may be the supernatural aid thereto, for it is God Himself, God Who infinitely transcends our created and finite being; nor do we always seek to appropriate that gift as fully as we might and could, because of sin and the vagrant desires of the heart. So we have the paradox that while the Christian life is an absolute receiving of God it is at the same time an advance towards Him, an ever-increasing possession of Him that we may be possessed by Him. 'My beloved is mine, and I am His.'

How, then, may we possess God and be possessed by Him? There are three steps on the way and the first is that of thought.

God has given us an intellect which may be used, and rightly used, for a variety of ends; we may use it for purely practical purposes to enable us to live, or for the satisfaction of our curiosity, or for the study of certain subjects, or for the understanding of

the world in which we live and the universe of
which it is a part. All those ends are legitimate but
secondary, the primary end for which the intellect is
created is that by it we might apprehend God Himself. For that reason God has revealed Himself to
us in terms which the intellect can grasp and deal
with.

If we would come to the possession of God we must
first of all think about Him and enter as deeply as
we may into the profundities of His revelation. Man
cannot evolve an adequate idea of God out of his
own inner consciousness, or even by the observation
of things created, but he can by thought understand
what God shows him of Himself and he must strive
to do so if his religion is to mean anything at all.

The Catholic Faith, as S. Thomas Aquinas
demonstrated centuries ago, is eminently rational,
and one of the facts which we have to rub into the
heads of our pagan friends who tell us that Christianity is irrational is that it is the most rational
thing in the world because it alone takes adequate
account of God. Philosophy is not enough, specula-
tive theology is not enough, it is revelation which
supplies our needs if we will make it our own; but
we must think.

God has given us a revelation which is eminently
reasonable, and a reasonable understanding of it
is a necessary foundation for anything further; a
reason for the faith that is in us is necessary not only
for purposes of apologetic but for the fullness of the
faith itself; there is no sort of justification for the
Catholic who deliberately avoids thinking out, as
well as he can, the truths of his faith. There are

people who say that so long as you try to love God
and lead a good life it does not matter what you
think, but that is nonsense, for your love and your
living alike depend upon what you think of God.
You must use your intellect for what it is worth.

The intellectual approach to God is necessary even
for those who have not got much intellect. Yet
when all is said and done it can only take us part
of the way to Him. This fact should not cause us
any disquiet, rather we should expect it, and that
for two reasons. First, because intellect and mind
are not convertible terms; the intellect is but one of
the powers of the mind (to use an old phrase) which
transcends it. Our most severe intellectual exercises
are seldom pure intellect; except perhaps in abstract
sciences like pure mathematics, there are always
intuitive processes at work which cannot be wholly
reduced to discursive thought; the most truly
original and deepest thinking is generally founded
not on intellectual demonstration alone but on
intuition as well. The intellect is not the only guide
to truth. There are truths which, while they are
reasonable in the sense of not being contrary to
reason, transcend the grasp of the intellect, and God
Who is Truth does so transcend it. The mind may
know Him, but the best the intellect can do is to
grasp certain truths about Him.

This leads us to our second reason for the finitude
of discursive thought, and that lies in the nature of
God Himself. The Athanasian Creed lays down
the truth that God is 'incomprehensible' in Himself.
That does not of course mean that we can know
nothing about Him, that would be to deny revelation

and the capability of the intellect to know the truth,
but it means that He is immeasurable (*immensus*).
Discursive thought proceeds by means of measure-
ment, comparison, and classification; but you cannot measure the infinite God, or compare Him to
His creatures. It is true that the eternal Son
came into the world to reveal God in terms of
our humanity, and He did so reveal Him; so we
can say that God is Father, but His Fatherhood
transcends all that can possibly be said of its
most perfect human counterpart; so we can say
that God is Love and Wisdom, but those qualities
in Him far transcend all that we can know. We
can say that a perfect man would be like God, we
can say that the Perfect Man is like God, but we
cannot say that God is like a perfect man; there is
always something over, and that an infinite something. Christ revealed so much, but there is so
much more which even He could not reveal because
we are incapable of grasping it. The finite creature
can never wholly comprehend the infinite God.
His Being must ever be a mystery hidden in light
unapproachable.

We must, then, use our intellects for what they
are worth, but not for more than they are worth.
We must think about God, even though our thought
takes us but a very little way, or we shall never comprehend Him at all, but our thought is only the first
step of the way; the second step is faith. By faith
we grasp what God gives us, we lay hold on God,
we trust God and the action of God because we know,
not only by intellectual demonstration but by
spiritual certainty, that He is and that He is good.

We have considered this way of faith elsewhere and there is no need to say much of it here; we must, however, note this—the further we go on in the spiritual life and the more knowledge God gives us of Himself the more we realize the deep truth of the Apostle's saying that 'we walk by faith, not by sight.'[1] We are guided to Him not only by the intellect's affirmations but much more by the mind's apprehension of Him, founded indeed upon those affirmations but reaching out beyond them by the intuitions of faith into the mystery of God's Being, which is for us both light and darkness.

There is a third and last step towards God which comes out of the second and completes it. You cannot really believe in God, you cannot begin to lay hold of Him by faith, without something else happening; you will begin to love Him. Thought leads to faith and faith to love irresistibly. God made us for Himself, He made us to love Him eternally, and the moment we really see Him there is a lighting up of that love. No soul can come within touch of God without beginning to love Him. I say beginning to love because at first that love will be mixed with other elements, indeed other elements will quite rightly persist; there will be, for instance, fear and penitence, but gradually all these will be subsumed so that they become facets of the one jewel, love.

When we begin to love God we not only apprehend Him we begin to possess Him; He gives Himself to our hearts so that we can say truly and wonderingly, 'My beloved is mine, and I am His.' We begin to

[1] 2 Cor. v. 7.

say not only 'O God,' which is the prayer of faith, but 'My God,' which is the prayer of love.

This is a very simple but a very beautiful experience. We come into church and kneel down in the presence of Jesus. We do not stop to think then, that has been done; we do not bother to analyse our feelings, that is unnecessary; but our faith goes out to Him, our love warms towards Him, we adore Him and are at peace. Very likely we do not say more than, 'My God, my Jesus,' and that is quite enough; in that moment we possess Him, we comprehend Him Who is incomprehensible, 'My beloved is mine, and I am His.'

How can this be? Well, listen to the words of an old writer of very great wisdom:

'All reasonable creatures, angel and man, have in them, each one by himself, one principal working power, the which is called a knowing power, and another principal working power, the which is called a loving power. Of the which two powers, to the first, the which is a knowing power, God Who is the Maker of them is ever more incomprehensible; but to the second, the which is the loving power, He is, in every man diversely, all comprehensible to the full. Insomuch that one loving soul alone in itself, by virtue of love, may comprehend in itself Him Who is sufficient to the full—and much more, without comparison—to fill all the souls and angels that may be. And this is the endless marvellous miracle of love, the working of which shall never have end, for ever shall He do it, and never shall He cease for to do it. See, whoso by grace see may; for the feeling of this is endless bliss, and the contrary is endless pain.' [1]

Our dear Lord when asked to define the great

[1] *Cloud of Unknowing*, chap. iv.

ommandment of the Law replied in the words of
Deuteronomy: 'Thou shalt love the Lord thy God
with all thy heart, and with all thy soul, and with
ll thy mind';[1] that is, with thy whole being.

So in the love of God alone is full satisfaction
because it alone satisfies our whole being, which was
made for just that. We are always running about
trying to find our satisfaction in loves that never
will satisfy because they only affect a part of our
being, or loves which only satisfy when held in union
with the love of God. The soul that has once been
touched by God's hand knows that there is nothing
in this world that is comparable to Him.

If the love of God is the love of our whole being
it is obviously something very much greater and
deeper than the love of emotion, it is much more than
fervour and is often most truly there when fervour
is absent; nevertheless we must not despise the love
of the emotions or try to repress it. Our love for God
goes through an emotional stage, just as the love of
a man for a maid does, but no true love is ever merely
emotional, still less is it that very horrid thing
emotionalism; at its most emotional it is always
something more.

Cynics are accustomed to sneer at the emotional
fervour of young lovers, but why? It is a very
beautiful and healthy thing and will never come
again; it is the outward manifestation of that love
which will later on settle down into something deeper
and more beautiful in Holy Marriage in which
there will still be a place for emotion. The fervour
of the young lover of God in like manner is beautiful

---

[1] S. Matt. xxii. 37; cf. Deut. vi. 5.

and healthy; it must by no means be crushed bu
used and offered, it is given by God for that purpos
But it must not be imagined that such fervour is th
same thing as the rapture of the saints, nor may
be cultivated for its own sake. It must be used fc
what it is worth and no more; it is given by Go
and must be given back to Him. The soul in ligh
must render to God the fervour which it feels; th
soul in darkness must love Him in a different an
more costing way; one is no more holy than th
other, they are different, that is all, and both alik
depend upon the gift of God Himself. There ma
be long periods during which the soul is consciou
of no emotion whatever, it seems just dry and cold
it loves God then by offering Him its poverty a
aforetime it offered its riches, and perhaps He find
poverty the richer gift after all.

If we love God with our whole being the intellec
and the mind find a place in that love, but above a
it is grounded in desire. 'All thy life now must a
ways stand in desire, if thou shalt advance in degre
of perfection. This desire must all ways be wrough
in thy will, by the hand of Almighty God and th
consent.'[1] The desire for God, the hunger of ou
hearts for Him, is the root of our love. Human lover
desire each other and when they cease to desire eacl
other they cease to love; it is no otherwise with th
love of God. But we must be sure that it is Goc
that we desire and nothing less. We sometime
mistake a desire for prayer or for the sensibl
realization for God for the desire for God Himsel
but in this way we are desiring His goods and no

[1] *Cloud of Unknowing*, chap. ii.

Himself, with disastrous results. If we would love
Him truly we must love Him for Himself, whatever
He gives or withholds, and if He come by the way
of darkness and hardness we must still desire Him;
so we shall find Him and no other way.

It is this desire for God which more than anything
else makes us like Him. As we have seen, most of
the trouble which we experience with the old man
arises from inordinate desires; as we come to desire
God truly so we desire Him above all else and every
other desire becomes subject to that primary one.
This does not of course mean that we shall never
desire anything else but God, nor that we shall never
desire wrongly, but it does mean that as our desire
for God grows no other desire can take the first
place but tends to find its place within the greater
one if it is right, or to be rejected if it is bad. By
desiring God we come to desire what He desires, and
so He makes us like Himself; for it is by our primary
desires that we are made.

God answers this desire by giving Himself to us
as our possession, He unites Himself to the very
depths of our being, He gives Himself to us in
such a way that we can say, 'My beloved is
mine.'

Some few years ago a learned theologian sought
to prove that there are in religion two sharply con-
trasted types of love—the one, to which he gives the
pagan name of ἔρως, seeking personal satisfaction
by possession; the other, to which he gives the
Christian name of ἀγάπη, being pure self-oblation;
whence he draws the conclusion that pure Christian
love is of the latter kind, which can only be perverted

and degraded by combination with the former.
I believe this argument to be thoroughly artificial
a typical product of the study, divorced from an
contact with experience.   Having regard only to it
own subject matter it would seem perilous to sugges
that no pagan had within him the beginnings o
ἀγάπη, nor can we truly say that S. Paul or S. Johη
were innocent of all trace of what this theologiaη
would call pagan love.   If we examine the phenome
non of Christian love we find it surely to consist no
in a separation of the one from the other, but in ι
combination of both.   So God gives Himself to us tο
be our possession, that is the joy of the Incarnatioη
and the comfort of the Blessed Sacrament.

Human love always desires to possess not becausο
it is selfish but because it is what it is; in theiη
several ways the lover desires to possess the beloved
the mother her child, the friend the friend, and Goc
Who has made us for Himself has made us of such
a kind that we may be able, creatures though we are,
to possess Him.   The Bible is a record of His self-
giving, and who are we to think ourselves superioη
to His gift?   Rather should we enter into it, rejoicε
in it, and seek to make ourselves in all ways worthy
of it.   The lives and writings of the saints are full
of this, and the Spiritual Marriage, so far from being
an unfortunate eroticism, is the most perfect possession of God possible on this earth to the perfectly
loving soul.

By love we enter into the possession of God, we
taste and see how gracious He is; but the perfect
possession of Him is possible only in heaven.   On

[1] Nygren, *Agape and Eros*.

earth He gives Himself to us in varying degrees, and
sometimes He seems to withdraw Himself from us;
nevertheless, He is ours and the loving soul possesses
Him. 'My beloved is mine' we can say with every
Communion that we make and every prayer that we
pray, and the realization of that gives joy to all our
living.

But there is more than this. God gives Himself
to us wholly and completely, and by love we possess
Him, but true love is never self-regarding, it is not
an inward-turning but an outward-going thing; the
purpose of the divine gift is not merely our enjoyment
of it. So the possession of God implies the donation
of self, indeed it is only so that it is possible; selfishness negates love and impedes possession.

There are plenty of devout people who are very
selfish indeed. They seek God for what they can
get out of Him; they go to church because they
enjoy the music or the ceremonial or the preaching,
or because they like the clergy; they pray because
it gives them satisfaction and do good works for the
same end; but there is no love there, they may seem
to others to love God but they do not do so, their
religion is a mere travesty of Christianity, a danger
to their own souls and an injury to the Church.
If the lover desires to possess the beloved he desires
even more to be possessed, and this involves the most
complete self-surrender of which he is capable. God
gives Himself perfectly to us, and our response must
be the gift of self to Him; so we seek to strip ourselves of everything selfish and self-willed. Because
we are His friends we desire not to follow our own
inclinations but to keep His commandments, for

He alone matters.   We desire that everything in us shall be pleasing to Him and nothing displeasing.

The love of God, then, issues in, and is expressed by, a deep devotion to His will; the surrender and consecration of self to that will, so that nothing else really matters or is to be compared with it.   So love becomes the spring of all our actions, the source of all virtues.   We do not pick up the Christian virtues one by one like pebbles on a beach; they may have to be developed singly but they all spring from love, and the more truly we are loving God the more we shall seek to be like Him and the more we shall be like Him.   'My beloved is mine,' truly, but also, 'I am His.'

So, then, the end of all our endeavour is that we may love God more and more, may open ourselves to Him that we may be filled with His love, and, being so filled, give ourselves to Him that that love may have free course in us and His will be accomplished in us.   So, and so only, shall we attain to the perfection which is His will for us.

CHAPTER X

THE LOVE OF MAN

*Thou shalt love the Lord thy God with all thy heart, and with
all thy soul, and with all thy mind. This is the first and
great commandment. And the second is like unto it, Thou
shalt love thy neighbour as thyself. On these two commandments hang all the law and the prophets.'*

S. MATT. xxii. 37-40.

OUR Lord Jesus Christ has made it quite clear
to us that the love of God with our whole being
is the first commandment of the law, not only for the
Jew but also for the Christian; the love of God is
indeed the purpose of our creation, so that this is not
only the first commandment but the great, the unique
one. 'Love and do what you will,' said S. Augustine, and although this maxim is patient of more
than one interpretation it is true since if our love of
God is right nothing else can be seriously wrong.

But our Lord has joined with this great commandment another one, 'Thou shalt love thy neighbour
as thyself.' This comes from a passage in Leviticus[1]
in which it occurs so incidentally that no one would
think of looking for it, or having found it by accident
would pay much attention to it. Yet our Lord takes
these two commands and, joining them together,
bases the whole of Christian living upon them. 'On

[1] Lev. xix. 18.

H

these two commandments hang all the law and the prophets,' these two represent the will of God for us without any ifs or buts whatsoever.

It is to these two loves that we as Christians are committed; it is God's will for us that we love Him with our whole being and our neighbour as ourselves. But how shall His will be obeyed? It is easy to love God for He is altogether lovely. We think of the perfection of God's beauty, of His love, of His holiness, and we must have a very hard heart indeed if we cannot feel at least some stirring to love Him. The beauty of creation, the love of human hearts, the perfect beauty and love of Jesus all lead us to the love of God;—but man! Man is so unpleasant, there is so much in him that is unlovely, so much that is downright bad, he is so stupid, so selfish, so cruel. Man is so antipathetic, there are so many people we do not like and who do not like us. Man is so disappointing; we do our best for a person for years and years and then he quite suddenly fails us completely and we say, 'What is the good of all my efforts?' All this terrible mess of humanity which we call the modern world, how on earth are we to love that?

But God makes neither demur nor reservation. 'Thou shalt love thy neighbour,' He says, and not only that but thou shalt love him 'as thyself.' Of course we do not, and that is one great reason why the Church is not the power in the world that she should be and the Sacred Heart is grieved by a predominantly godless civilization, for you cannot calmly ignore a fundamental command of God without producing sad consequences. God has said

'Thou shalt love thy neighbour as thyself,' and we
do not do it, perhaps we go further and say we
cannot do it. Obviously there is something which
needs looking into there.

In the first place we have to realize that the love
of man which our dear Lord would see in us is after
all not ours but His. It is not natural affection
which God would have us show to all and sundry,
that would indeed hardly be worth having, but a
much greater and more beautiful thing—supernatural
charity, the very love of God Himself given to us to
minister to our fellow men.

That fact emerges very clearly for those who have
eyes to see it in the beautiful parable with which our
Lord illustrates this very saying—the parable of the
Good Samaritan. What we see quite clearly there
is that the Good Samaritan was not bubbling over
with affection for the man by the wayside but was
filled with charity towards him.

Why did our Lord deliberately lay stress upon the
nationality of the Good Samaritan? Why did He
deliberately say he was not a Jew? Just, I think, to
bring out this fact. The Jews regarded themselves
as a superior race to the outcast Samaritans and
treated them with the utmost contempt. 'How is it,'
said the woman at the well to our Lord with surprise,
'that Thou, being a Jew, askest drink of me, which am
a woman of Samaria?' That indicates the state of
affairs, and that sort of treatment naturally produced
in the Samaritans what we in our tiresome psycho-
logical jargon call an 'inferiority complex,' with the
result that they hated the Jews very thoroughly. We
have no reason to suppose that this particular Samari-

tan hated the Jew by the roadside, but he certainly
had no reason to love him, there was every possible
excuse for him to pass by on the other side as the
man's compatriots had done before him; but because he was moved by the beautiful charity of God
he did what they would not do and poured out upon
him, not a little human affection or sympathy, but
the very love of God.

Mr. Thomas Derrick has caught this point exactly
in his brilliant and arresting book of drawings called
The Prodigal Son and other Parables. In this book the
artist has taken certain of the parables and illustrated
them in terms of modern life. So the man who fell
among thieves is a young business man who has been
set upon by roughs and left at the roadside to die.
Then the priest hurries by, fearful lest he be
drawn into something unpleasant; the Nonconformist
minister stops, perhaps to murmur 'the wages of sin
is death,' and goes his way. Then along comes a little
Jewish commercial traveller in an old Ford car
loaded up with boxes, stops and goes to the man in
trouble. It is the Jew helping the Gentile here, not
vice versa, but it is a very close parallel in terms of
modern civilization of what our Lord intended to
imply by His Samaritan—divine charity poured out
upon a man one has no cause to love, a man who in
other circumstances would probably despise one.

If we are going to set out to like every one we
meet we shall never do it. We shall like certain
people because they have something in common with
us or are otherwise admirable, others we shall dislike
for various reasons; but God asks us to love, not to
like, and to love all, even those who despise us, and

not some. This is truly impossible to our little
human loving, but God gives us far more than that,
for He gives the infused virtue of charity, His own
charity, and He gives it to us in order that we may
give it back to Him and pass it on to our neighbours.
Therein lies the vocation of us all, that is the balm
which Christ brings through us to a bruised humanity
—the oil, and we must add to it our own little bit of
goodwill, wine truly but sometimes a little sour.

If our love for our neighbour is God's love it is
also moved by our love for God. Charity is one
thing and not two; charity to man is not different
from charity to God, but it flows from it. A
philanthropist may do a great deal of good but even
so he is a far smaller person than a Christian saint
because he is essentially humanist; he is genuinely
interested in humanity and sympathetic to the unfortunate, and so he tries to do his best for them,
but that best is limited by its outlook, it is the milk
of human kindness not the oil of the love of God.

Saints have often been most philanthropic and
have done more than most philanthropists in the
relief of human suffering; they have given what the
philanthropist can never give, divine charity itself,
warming the soul and leading it to the Heart of God,
and they have done that not only because they loved
man but much more because they loved God. If
we are to love our neighbour as God would have us
love him it is because we love God Himself above all,
and find Him in man and man in Him, and because we
love man as He loves him, so that God is loving him
through and in us.

What miracles might not the Church of God do if

only we would rise to the greatness of divine charity
and not allow ourselves to be cribbed, cabined, and
confined in our petty likes and dislikes! 'See how
these Christians love one another!' See how they
love all men as themselves! What a vision! If
only they did! And why do they not? Why do *we*
not?

Primarily because we are so little disciplined in
regard to people. We dislike so many, and our
dislikes are due in nine cases out of ten to selfishness,
though we can always persuade ourselves that they
are due to something else. The trouble is that we
naturally look upon others in regard to the effect that
they have upon ourselves, either they attract us or
they repel us and we react instinctively; but until
we can get our ego out of our relationships (which is
a matter of very strong and close interior mortification) we are not going to get divine charity in.
That is why it is so important to love our neighbour
in God. If one simply likes or dislikes him for himself alone then inevitably one's ego gets in the way;
we have to learn to see our neighbour in God and
eliminate self-interest if we are to love him as God
would have us love him. This means an ever-
deepening detachment from people in themselves
and in relation to ourselves.

This detachment is a very necessary thing, but it is
not the end, we have to be detached from people in
themselves that we may find them in God, and until
we so find them we have not charity towards them,
for charity is no negative thing but the most positive
thing there is.

One sometimes comes across very holy people

who are as hard as marble and as cold as ice; they
have learnt the lesson of detachment, mostly at
very great cost, but they are arrested there, they have
got no further and so missed the most important
thing; they have merely killed natural affection
without arriving at supernatural charity. Detachment has been carried to its very end, but they have
gone no further and have only succeeded in becom-
ing heartless. Detachment is necessary that the
love of God may shine through us, that we may cease
to dislike people because they are antipathetic or
disappointing, because they dislike or hurt us or
even some one else whom we love, and that we may
love them in God and He may love them through
us; but even so we shall rightly love some people more
than others, for natural affection should not be
crushed but broadened and deepened and perfected,
the supernatural gift bringing the natural to its full
stature, not destroying it. It is the selfishness which
must be destroyed.

So, then, God gives us a high and glorious charity
which we can show forth to others, and which we
must show forth independently of our natural likes
and dislikes, charity perfecting our personal love.
What are the marks of this charity?

First of all sympathy, or, if you will, compassion.
The Good Samaritan is primarily a picture of our
Lord Himself, the perfect exemplar of divine charity,
and of Him it is recorded that He had compassion
on the multitude. That compassion was not shown
by standing above them and improving them from
without; it was shown, as the word implies, by
coming right down to their level, entering into their

hearts and suffering with them, rejoicing with them, feeling with them, thinking with them. People do not like being improved, but they will respond to sympathy, the sympathy of Christ in us.

Here my mind goes back to the little Jew, for Mr. Derrick makes a very subtle point here. The priest and the Levite were walking along the road, the Jew came in a car, but no sooner does he see the man by the roadside than he jams on his brakes and jumps as quickly as ever he can out of the car to run to his aid. Now if you are walking you are mixed up with every one else in the street, in a car you are separated from them; if you are walking it is easy and natural to stop and look at anything which catches your attention, but in a car it involves an effort to stop; but the Good Samaritan here refuses to be separated, he makes the effort instantly and naturally, he enters right into the poor man's sufferings and comes right down to his side to do it, and then he goes to him and without any fuss produces just what is needed, oil and wine, and binds up his wounds. That is the first step to the wounded man's recovery.

But sympathy by itself, beautiful though it be, is not enough, there must be something more—benevolence. Now benevolence is one of those words (like charity itself) which have come down in the world; in common parlance it is almost equivalent to a rather vague form of well-wishing. But it does not mean that, it means goodwill. To have goodwill towards a person we must have eliminated our evil will, and did charity mean no more than this it would mean something very beautiful: for peace, the peace of God, is, as the angels have told us, for men of good-will. But benevolence means more than this, it means that we really will the perfect good of our neighbour and will it so strongly that we are prepared to take trouble about it.

Look at the Good Samaritan: he willed the good of the man by the wayside so strongly that he came to his assistance at real personal risk. He was a busy man, but he not only bound up his wounds but went out of his way to take him to an inn and stay with him till he was out of danger. Mr. Derrick's picture of the ugly little man sitting by the bedside with his toes turned in, twiddling his thumbs and smiling at the invalid, is full of true charity. He would not leave him until he had done all he could for his true good.

If we were prepared to be benevolent in this sense to our neighbours there would be no question about our love for them, for benevolence is not merely the fruit of love, it augments it. The best way to love a person is to go to some trouble to aid him towards a worthy end.

And the third mark of charity, a mark which interpenetrates both the others and makes them real, is sacrifice. We have no reason to suppose that the Good Samaritan was at all well off as regards this world's goods and the two pence (which Mr. Derrick aptly translates into treasury notes) must have meant a good deal to him; nevertheless he gave them readily and gladly because they were necessary to the sick man's recovery. There must always be a readiness for personal sacrifice in the love of our neighbour; it varies in kind, it may be of time, energy, comfort, spiritual things as well as temporal, but it must always be there colouring the whole of life; the self-giving of love which is the complete antithesis of selfishness.

Our Lord tells us that we are to love our neighbour as ourselves. There is nothing selfish in the true love of oneself for it is expressed in the surrender of that self to God; so also the love of our neighbour is expressed in sacrifice. The love of our neighbour must be marked with the cross.

'As My Father hath sent Me even so send I you.'[1] These words were spoken by our Lord to the Apostles, but there is a sense in which they are true of every member of His Church. We are here not merely to save our own souls but to be Christ to the world; He fills us with the riches of His grace, not merely for our own benefit that we may enjoy Him, but that we may fulfil His purpose; He makes us members of His Body that through us that Body may fulfil the purpose of its existence.

On Ascension Day the physical presence of the Son of God in this world came to an end, but He is still incarnate in the world in His Body the Church, and in that incarnation we have our place. Christ is in this world in His Church for the same purpose that He came in the flesh; the Church is here to do what He did, to love men, to promote His will for them, to bring them to the feet of God. We are sent truly to be Christ to the world.

We live in a dark and troubled age, men of goodwill are turning about uncertain of their way, bitterly conscious of the failure of all that makes up

[1] S. John xx. 21.

civilization to accomplish its purpose, seeking des-
pairingly for new lights; yet there stands among us
One Who says, 'I am the Light of the World,' and
we know in our hearts that He is. He holds the
keys to our riddles, He can regenerate our bad nature
and deliver us from the madness of the dark, He
can bring us to fullness of life and God.

But how does He will to do this? Through His
Body, in the last resort through us. For if He has
said, 'I am the Light of the World,'[1] He has also said
and in the same sense, 'Ye are the light of the
world,'[2] a light not self-generated but a flame of
the light of Christ. Our business is to go forth
bearing the Light of the World in the lanterns of
our hearts, and if we would only do it the whole of
humanity would be irradiated. Men do not 'light
a candle and put it under a bushel, but on a candle-
stick; and it giveth light unto all that are in the
house.'[3] We are sent to be Christ to the world,
and nothing else will serve. There is no place for
self-centred religion. If the light is to shine forth, it
will be through charity all-embracing; the charity
of men sent from God, filled with the Spirit of Christ
and His love, to bring the world home to the Heart
of God.

[1] ibid., viii. 12.   [2] S. Matt. v. 14.
[3] ibid., v. 15.

Printed in Great Britain by
A. R. Mowbray & Co. Limited
London and Oxford   71024